OECD/G20 Base Erosion and Profit Shifting Project

Transfer Pricing Documentation and Country-by-Country Reporting, Action 13 - 2015 Final Report

This document and any map included herein are without prejudice to the status of or sovereignty over any territory, to the delimitation of international frontiers and boundaries and to the name of any territory, city or area.

Please cite this publication as:
OECD (2015), *Transfer Pricing Documentation and Country-by-Country Reporting, Action 13 - 2015 Final Report*, OECD/G20 Base Erosion and Profit Shifting Project, OECD Publishing, Paris.
http://dx.doi.org/10.1787/9789264241480-en

ISBN 978-92-64-24146-6 (print)
ISBN 978-92-64-24148-0 (PDF)

Series: OECD/G20 Base Erosion and Profit Shifting Project
ISSN 2313-2604 (print)
ISSN 2313-2612 (online)

Photo credits: Cover © ninog – Fotolia.com

Corrigenda to OECD publications may be found on line at: *www.oecd.org/about/publishing/corrigenda.htm*.

Foreword

International tax issues have never been as high on the political agenda as they are today. The integration of national economies and markets has increased substantially in recent years, putting a strain on the international tax rules, which were designed more than a century ago. Weaknesses in the current rules create opportunities for base erosion and profit shifting (BEPS), requiring bold moves by policy makers to restore confidence in the system and ensure that profits are taxed where economic activities take place and value is created.

Following the release of the report *Addressing Base Erosion and Profit Shifting* in February 2013, OECD and G20 countries adopted a 15-point Action Plan to address BEPS in September 2013. The Action Plan identified 15 actions along three key pillars: introducing coherence in the domestic rules that affect cross-border activities, reinforcing substance requirements in the existing international standards, and improving transparency as well as certainty.

Since then, all G20 and OECD countries have worked on an equal footing and the European Commission also provided its views throughout the BEPS project. Developing countries have been engaged extensively via a number of different mechanisms, including direct participation in the Committee on Fiscal Affairs. In addition, regional tax organisations such as the African Tax Administration Forum, the *Centre de rencontre des administrations fiscales* and the *Centro Interamericano de Administraciones Tributarias*, joined international organisations such as the International Monetary Fund, the World Bank and the United Nations, in contributing to the work. Stakeholders have been consulted at length: in total, the BEPS project received more than 1 400 submissions from industry, advisers, NGOs and academics. Fourteen public consultations were held, streamed live on line, as were webcasts where the OECD Secretariat periodically updated the public and answered questions.

After two years of work, the 15 actions have now been completed. All the different outputs, including those delivered in an interim form in 2014, have been consolidated into a comprehensive package. The BEPS package of measures represents the first substantial renovation of the international tax rules in almost a century. Once the new measures become applicable, it is expected that profits will be reported where the economic activities that generate them are carried out and where value is created. BEPS planning strategies that rely on outdated rules or on poorly co-ordinated domestic measures will be rendered ineffective.

Implementation therefore becomes key at this stage. The BEPS package is designed to be implemented via changes in domestic law and practices, and via treaty provisions, with negotiations for a multilateral instrument under way and expected to be finalised in 2016. OECD and G20 countries have also agreed to continue to work together to ensure a consistent and co-ordinated implementation of the BEPS recommendations. Globalisation requires that global solutions and a global dialogue be established which go beyond OECD and G20 countries. To further this objective, in 2016 OECD and G20 countries will conceive an inclusive framework for monitoring, with all interested countries participating on an equal footing.

A better understanding of how the BEPS recommendations are implemented in practice could reduce misunderstandings and disputes between governments. Greater focus on implementation and tax administration should therefore be mutually beneficial to governments and business. Proposed improvements to data and analysis will help support ongoing evaluation of the quantitative impact of BEPS, as well as evaluating the impact of the countermeasures developed under the BEPS Project.

Table of contents

Abbreviations and acronyms

APA	Advance pricing agreement
BEPS	Base erosion and profit shifting
CAA	Competent authority agreement
CbC	Country-by-Country
DTC	Double tax convention
FTE	Full-time equivalent
G20	Group of twenty
MAP	Mutual agreement procedure
MCAA	Multilateral competent authority agreement
MNE	Multinational enterprise
OECD	Organisation for Economic Co-operation and Development
PE	Permanent establishment
R&D	Research and development
SME	Small and medium-sized enterprise
TIEA	Tax information exchange agreement
XML	Extensible markup language

Executive summary

This report contains revised standards for transfer pricing documentation and a template for Country-by-Country Reporting of income, taxes paid and certain measures of economic activity.

Action 13 of the *Action Plan on Base Erosion and Profit Shifting* (BEPS Action Plan, OECD, 2013) requires the development of "*rules regarding transfer pricing documentation to enhance transparency for tax administration, taking into consideration the compliance costs for business. The rules to be developed will include a requirement that MNEs provide all relevant governments with needed information on their global allocation of the income, economic activity and taxes paid among countries according to a common template*".

In response to this requirement, a three-tiered standardised approach to transfer pricing documentation has been developed.

First, the guidance on transfer pricing documentation requires multinational enterprises (MNEs) to provide tax administrations with high-level information regarding their global business operations and transfer pricing policies in a "master file" that is to be available to all relevant tax administrations.

Second, it requires that detailed transactional transfer pricing documentation be provided in a "local file" specific to each country, identifying material related party transactions, the amounts involved in those transactions, and the company's analysis of the transfer pricing determinations they have made with regard to those transactions.

Third, large MNEs are required to file a Country-by-Country Report that will provide annually and for each tax jurisdiction in which they do business the amount of revenue, profit before income tax and income tax paid and accrued. It also requires MNEs to report their number of employees, stated capital, retained earnings and tangible assets in each tax jurisdiction. Finally, it requires MNEs to identify each entity within the group doing business in a particular tax jurisdiction and to provide an indication of the business activities each entity engages in.

Taken together, these three documents (master file, local file and Country-by-Country Report) will require taxpayers to articulate consistent transfer pricing positions and will provide tax administrations with useful information to assess transfer pricing risks, make determinations about where audit resources can most effectively be deployed, and, in the event audits are called for, provide information to commence and target audit enquiries. This information should make it easier for tax administrations to identify whether companies have engaged in transfer pricing and other practices that have the effect of artificially shifting substantial amounts of income into tax-advantaged environments. The countries participating in the BEPS project agree that these new reporting provisions, and the transparency they will encourage, will contribute to the objective of understanding, controlling, and tackling BEPS behaviours.

The specific content of the various documents reflects an effort to balance tax administration information needs, concerns about inappropriate use of the information, and the compliance costs and burdens imposed on business. Some countries would strike that balance in a different way by requiring reporting in the Country-by-Country Report of additional transactional data (beyond that available in the master file and local file for transactions of entities operating in their jurisdictions) regarding related party interest payments, royalty payments and especially related party service fees. Countries expressing this view are primarily those from emerging markets (Argentina, Brazil, People's Republic of China, Colombia, India, Mexico, South Africa, and Turkey) who state they need such information to perform risk assessment and who find it challenging to obtain information on the global operations of an MNE group headquartered elsewhere. Other countries expressed support for the way in which the balance has been struck in this document. Taking all these views into account, it is mandated that countries participating in the BEPS project will carefully review the implementation of these new standards and will reassess no later than the end of 2020 whether modifications to the content of these reports should be made to require reporting of additional or different data.

Consistent and effective implementation of the transfer pricing documentation standards and in particular of the Country-by-Country Report is essential. Therefore, countries participating in the OECD/G20 BEPS Project agreed on the core elements of the implementation of transfer pricing documentation and Country-by-Country Reporting. This agreement calls for the master file and the local file to be delivered by MNEs directly to local tax administrations. Country-by-Country Reports should be filed in the jurisdiction of tax residence of the ultimate parent entity and shared between jurisdictions through automatic exchange of information, pursuant to government-to-government mechanisms such as the multilateral Convention on Mutual Administrative Assistance in Tax Matters, bilateral tax treaties or tax information exchange agreements (TIEAs). In limited circumstances, secondary mechanisms, including local filing can be used as a backup.

These new Country-by-Country Reporting requirements are to be implemented for fiscal years beginning on or after 1 January 2016 and apply, subject to the 2020 review, to MNEs with annual consolidated group revenue equal to or exceeding EUR 750 million. It is acknowledged that some jurisdictions may need time to follow their particular domestic legislative process in order to make necessary adjustments to the law.

In order to facilitate the implementation of the new reporting standards, an implementation package has been developed consisting of model legislation which could be used by countries to require MNE groups to file the Country-by-Country Report and competent authority agreements that are to be used to facilitate implementation of the exchange of those reports among tax administrations. As a next step, it is intended that an XML Schema and a related User Guide will be developed with a view to accommodating the electronic exchange of Country-by-Country Reports.

It is recognised that the need for more effective dispute resolution may increase as a result of the enhanced risk assessment capability following the adoption and implementation of a Country-by-Country Reporting requirement. This need has been addressed when designing government-to-government mechanisms to be used to facilitate the automatic exchange of Country-by-Country Reports.

Jurisdictions endeavour to introduce, as necessary, domestic legislation in a timely manner. They are also encouraged to expand the coverage of their international agreements for exchange of information. Mechanisms will be developed to monitor jurisdictions' compliance with their commitments and to monitor the effectiveness of the filing and dissemination mechanisms. The outcomes of this monitoring will be taken into consideration in the 2020 review.

Chapter V of the Transfer Pricing Guidelines on Documentation

The text of Chapter V of the Transfer Pricing Guidelines is deleted in its entirety and replaced with the following language and annexes.

A. Introduction

1. This chapter provides guidance for tax administrations to take into account in developing rules and/or procedures on documentation to be obtained from taxpayers in connection with a transfer pricing enquiry or risk assessment. It also provides guidance to assist taxpayers in identifying documentation that would be most helpful in showing that their transactions satisfy the arm's length principle and hence in resolving transfer pricing issues and facilitating tax examinations.

2. When Chapter V of these Guidelines was adopted in 1995, tax administrations and taxpayers had less experience in creating and using transfer pricing documentation. The previous language in Chapter V of the Guidelines put an emphasis on the need for reasonableness in the documentation process from the perspective of both taxpayers and tax administrations, as well as on the desire for a greater level of cooperation between tax administrations and taxpayers in addressing documentation issues in order to avoid excessive documentation compliance burdens while at the same time providing for adequate information to apply the arm's length principle reliably. The previous language of Chapter V did not provide for a list of documents to be included in a transfer pricing documentation package nor did it provide clear guidance with respect to the link between the process for documenting transfer pricing, the administration of penalties and the burden of proof.

3. Since then, many countries have adopted transfer pricing documentation rules and the proliferation of these requirements, combined with a dramatic increase in the volume and complexity of international intra-group trade and the heightened scrutiny of transfer pricing issues by tax administrations, has resulted in a significant increase in compliance costs for taxpayers. Nevertheless tax administrations often find transfer pricing documentation to be less than fully informative and not adequate for their tax enforcement and risk assessment needs.

4. The following discussion identifies three objectives of transfer pricing documentation rules. The discussion also provides guidance for the development of such rules so that transfer pricing compliance is more straightforward and more consistent among countries, while at the same time providing tax administrations with more focused and useful information for transfer pricing risk assessments and audits. An important overarching consideration in developing such rules is to balance the usefulness of the data to tax administrations for transfer pricing risk assessment and other purposes with any increased compliance burdens placed on taxpayers. In this respect it is noted that clear and widely

adopted documentation rules can reduce compliance costs which could otherwise arise in a transfer pricing dispute.

B. Objectives of transfer pricing documentation requirements

5. Three objectives of transfer pricing documentation are:

1. to ensure that taxpayers give appropriate consideration to transfer pricing requirements in establishing prices and other conditions for transactions between associated enterprises and in reporting the income derived from such transactions in their tax returns;
2. to provide tax administrations with the information necessary to conduct an informed transfer pricing risk assessment; and
3. to provide tax administrations with useful information to employ in conducting an appropriately thorough audit of the transfer pricing practices of entities subject to tax in their jurisdiction, although it may be necessary to supplement the documentation with additional information as the audit progresses.

6. Each of these objectives should be considered in designing appropriate domestic transfer pricing documentation requirements. It is important that taxpayers be required to carefully evaluate, at or before the time of filing a tax return, their own compliance with the applicable transfer pricing rules. It is also important that tax administrations be able to access the information they need to conduct a transfer pricing risk assessment to make an informed decision about whether to perform an audit. In addition, it is important that tax administrations be able to access or demand, on a timely basis, all additional information necessary to conduct a comprehensive audit once the decision to conduct such an audit is made.

B.1. Taxpayer's assessment of its compliance with the arm's length principle

7. By requiring taxpayers to articulate convincing, consistent and cogent transfer pricing positions, transfer pricing documentation can help to ensure that a culture of compliance is created. Well-prepared documentation will give tax administrations some assurance that the taxpayer has analysed the positions it reports on tax returns, has considered the available comparable data, and has reached consistent transfer pricing positions. Moreover, contemporaneous documentation requirements will help to ensure the integrity of the taxpayers' positions and restrain taxpayers from developing justifications for their positions after the fact.

8. This compliance objective may be supported in two important ways. First, tax administrations can require that transfer pricing documentation requirements be satisfied on a contemporaneous basis. This would mean that the documentation would be prepared at the time of the transaction, or in any event, no later than the time of completing and filing the tax return for the fiscal year in which the transaction takes place. The second way to encourage compliance is to establish transfer pricing penalty regimes in a manner intended to reward timely and accurate preparation of transfer pricing documentation and to create incentives for timely, careful consideration of the taxpayer's transfer pricing positions. Filing requirements and penalty provisions related to documentation are discussed in greater detail in Section D, below.

9. While ideally taxpayers will use transfer pricing documentation as an opportunity to articulate a well thought-out basis for their transfer pricing policies, thereby meeting an important objective of such requirements, issues such as costs, time constraints, and competing demands for the attention of relevant personnel can sometimes undermine these objectives. It is therefore important for countries to keep documentation requirements reasonable and focused on material transactions in order to ensure mindful attention to the most important matters.

B.2. Transfer pricing risk assessment

10. Effective risk identification and assessment constitute an essential early stage in the process of selecting appropriate cases for transfer pricing audits or enquiries and in focusing such audits on the most important issues. Because tax administrations operate with limited resources, it is important for them to accurately evaluate, at the very outset of a possible audit, whether a taxpayer's transfer pricing arrangements warrant in-depth review and a commitment of significant tax enforcement resources. Particularly with regard to transfer pricing issues (which generally are complex and fact-intensive), effective risk assessment becomes an essential prerequisite for a focused and resource-efficient audit. The OECD Handbook on Transfer Pricing Risk Assessment is a useful tool to consider in conducting such risk assessments.

11. Proper assessment of transfer pricing risk by the tax administration requires access to sufficient, relevant and reliable information at an early stage. While there are many sources of relevant information, transfer pricing documentation is one critical source of such information.

12. There is a variety of tools and sources of information used for identifying and evaluating transfer pricing risks of taxpayers and transactions, including transfer pricing forms (to be filed with the annual tax return), transfer pricing mandatory questionnaires focusing on particular areas of risk, general transfer pricing documentation requirements identifying the supporting evidence necessary to demonstrate the taxpayer's compliance with the arm's length principle, and cooperative discussions between tax administrations and taxpayers. Each of the tools and sources of information appears to respond to the same fundamental observation: there is a need for the tax administration to have ready access to relevant information at an early stage to enable an accurate and informed transfer pricing risk assessment. Assuring that a high quality transfer pricing risk assessment can be carried out efficiently and with the right kinds of reliable information should be one important consideration in designing transfer pricing documentation rules.

B.3. Transfer pricing audit

13. A third objective for transfer pricing documentation is to provide tax administrations with useful information to employ in conducting a thorough transfer pricing audit. Transfer pricing audit cases tend to be fact-intensive. They often involve difficult evaluations of the comparability of several transactions and markets. They can require detailed consideration of financial, factual and other industry information. The availability of adequate information from a variety of sources during the audit is critical to facilitating a tax administration's orderly examination of the taxpayer's controlled transactions with associated enterprises and enforcement of the applicable transfer pricing rules.

14. In situations where a proper transfer pricing risk assessment suggests that a thorough transfer pricing audit is warranted with regard to one or more issues, it is clearly the case

that the tax administration must have the ability to obtain, within a reasonable period, all of the relevant documents and information in the taxpayer's possession. This includes information regarding the taxpayer's operations and functions, relevant information on the operations, functions and financial results of associated enterprises with which the taxpayer has entered into controlled transactions, information regarding potential comparables, including internal comparables, and documents regarding the operations and financial results of potentially comparable uncontrolled transactions and unrelated parties. To the extent such information is included in the transfer pricing documentation, special information and document production procedures can potentially be avoided. It must be recognised, however, that it would be unduly burdensome and inefficient for transfer pricing documentation to attempt to anticipate all of the information that might possibly be required for a full audit. Accordingly, situations will inevitably arise when tax administrations wish to obtain information not included in the documentation package. Thus, a tax administration's access to information should not be limited to, or by, the documentation package relied on in a transfer pricing risk assessment. Where a jurisdiction requires particular information to be kept for transfer pricing audit purposes, such requirements should balance the tax administration's need for information and the compliance burdens on taxpayers.

15. It may often be the case that the documents and other information required for a transfer pricing audit will be in the possession of members of the MNE group other than the local affiliate under examination. Often the necessary documents will be located outside the country whose tax administration is conducting the audit. It is therefore important that the tax administration is able to obtain directly or through information sharing, such as exchange of information mechanisms, information that extends beyond the country's borders.

C. A three-tiered approach to transfer pricing documentation

16. In order to achieve the objectives described in Section B, countries should adopt a standardised approach to transfer pricing documentation. This section describes a three-tiered structure consisting of (i) a master file containing standardised information relevant for all MNE group members; (ii) a local file referring specifically to material transactions of the local taxpayer; and (iii) a Country-by-Country Report containing certain information relating to the global allocation of the MNE's income and taxes paid together with certain indicators of the location of economic activity within the MNE group.

17. This approach to transfer pricing documentation will provide tax administrations with relevant and reliable information to perform an efficient and robust transfer pricing risk assessment analysis. It will also provide a platform on which the information necessary for an audit can be developed and provide taxpayers with a means and an incentive to meaningfully consider and describe their compliance with the arm's length principle in material transactions.

C.1. Master file

18. The master file should provide an overview of the MNE group business, including the nature of its global business operations, its overall transfer pricing policies, and its global allocation of income and economic activity in order to assist tax administrations in evaluating the presence of significant transfer pricing risk. In general, the master file is intended to provide a high-level overview in order to place the MNE group's transfer

pricing practices in their global economic, legal, financial and tax context. It is not intended to require exhaustive listings of minutiae (e.g. a listing of every patent owned by members of the MNE group) as this would be both unnecessarily burdensome and inconsistent with the objectives of the master file. In producing the master file, including lists of important agreements, intangibles and transactions, taxpayers should use prudent business judgment in determining the appropriate level of detail for the information supplied, keeping in mind the objective of the master file to provide tax administrations a high-level overview of the MNE's global operations and policies. When the requirements of the master file can be fully satisfied by specific cross-references to other existing documents, such cross-references, together with copies of the relevant documents, should be deemed to satisfy the relevant requirement. For purposes of producing the master file, information is considered important if its omission would affect the reliability of the transfer pricing outcomes.

19. The information required in the master file provides a "blueprint" of the MNE group and contains relevant information that can be grouped in five categories: a) the MNE group's organisational structure; b) a description of the MNE's business or businesses; c) the MNE's intangibles; d) the MNE's intercompany financial activities; and (e) the MNE's financial and tax positions.

20. Taxpayers should present the information in the master file for the MNE as a whole. However, organisation of the information presented by line of business is permitted where well justified by the facts, e.g. where the structure of the MNE group is such that some significant business lines operate largely independently or are recently acquired. Where line of business presentation is used, care should be taken to assure that centralised group functions and transactions between business lines are properly described in the master file. Even where line of business presentation is selected, the entire master file consisting of all business lines should be available to each country in order to assure that an appropriate overview of the MNE group's global business is provided.

21. Annex I to Chapter V of these Guidelines sets out the information to be included in the master file.

C.2. Local file

22. In contrast to the master file, which provides a high-level overview as described in paragraph 18, the local file provides more detailed information relating to specific intercompany transactions. The information required in the local file supplements the master file and helps to meet the objective of assuring that the taxpayer has complied with the arm's length principle in its material transfer pricing positions affecting a specific jurisdiction. The local file focuses on information relevant to the transfer pricing analysis related to transactions taking place between a local country affiliate and associated enterprises in different countries and which are material in the context of the local country's tax system. Such information would include relevant financial information regarding those specific transactions, a comparability analysis, and the selection and application of the most appropriate transfer pricing method. Where a requirement of the local file can be fully satisfied by a specific cross-reference to information contained in the master file, such a cross-reference should suffice.

23. Annex II to Chapter V of these Guidelines sets out the items of information to be included in the local file.

C.3. Country-by-Country Report

24. The Country-by-Country Report requires aggregate tax jurisdiction-wide information relating to the global allocation of the income, the taxes paid, and certain indicators of the location of economic activity among tax jurisdictions in which the MNE group operates. The report also requires a listing of all the Constituent Entities for which financial information is reported, including the tax jurisdiction of incorporation, where different from the tax jurisdiction of residence, as well as the nature of the main business activities carried out by that Constituent Entity.

25. The Country-by-Country Report will be helpful for high-level transfer pricing risk assessment purposes. It may also be used by tax administrations in evaluating other BEPS related risks and where appropriate for economic and statistical analysis. However, the information in the Country-by-Country Report should not be used as a substitute for a detailed transfer pricing analysis of individual transactions and prices based on a full functional analysis and a full comparability analysis. The information in the Country-by-Country Report on its own does not constitute conclusive evidence that transfer prices are or are not appropriate. It should not be used by tax administrations to propose transfer pricing adjustments based on a global formulary apportionment of income.

26. Annex III to Chapter V of these Guidelines contains a model template for the Country-by-Country Report together with its accompanying instructions.

D. Compliance issues

D.1. Contemporaneous documentation

27. Each taxpayer should endeavour to determine transfer prices for tax purposes in accordance with the arm's length principle, based upon information reasonably available at the time of the transaction. Thus, a taxpayer ordinarily should give consideration to whether its transfer pricing is appropriate for tax purposes before the pricing is established and should confirm the arm's length nature of its financial results at the time of filing its tax return.

28. Taxpayers should not be expected to incur disproportionately high costs and burdens in producing documentation. Therefore, tax administrations should balance requests for documentation against the expected cost and administrative burden to the taxpayer of creating it. Where a taxpayer reasonably demonstrates, having regard to the principles of these Guidelines, that either no comparable data exists or that the cost of locating the comparable data would be disproportionately high relative to the amounts at issue, the taxpayer should not be required to incur costs in searching for such data.

D.2. Time frame

29. Practices regarding the timing of the preparation of the documentation differ among countries. Some countries require information to be finalised by the time the tax return is filed. Others require documentation to be in place by the time the audit commences. There is also a variety in practice regarding the amount of time given to taxpayers to respond to specific tax administration requests for documentation and other audit related information requests. These differences in the time requirements for providing information can add to taxpayers' difficulties in setting priorities and in providing the right information to the tax administrations at the right time.

30. The best practice is to require that the local file be finalised no later than the due date for the filing of the tax return for the fiscal year in question. The master file should be reviewed and, if necessary, updated by the tax return due date for the ultimate parent of the MNE group. In countries pursuing policies of auditing transactions as they occur under co-operative compliance programmes, it may be necessary for certain information to be provided in advance of the filing of the tax return.

31. With regard to the Country-by-Country Report, it is recognised that in some instances final statutory financial statements and other financial information that may be relevant for the country-by-country data described in Annex III may not be finalised until after the due date for tax returns in some countries for a given fiscal year. Under the given circumstances, the date for completion of the Country-by-Country Report described in Annex III to Chapter V of these Guidelines may be extended to one year following the last day of the fiscal year of the ultimate parent of the MNE group.

D.3. Materiality

32. Not all transactions that occur between associated enterprises are sufficiently material to require full documentation in the local file. Tax administrations have an interest in seeing the most important information while at the same time they also have an interest in seeing that MNEs are not so overwhelmed with compliance demands that they fail to consider and document the most important items. Thus, individual country transfer pricing documentation requirements based on Annex II to Chapter V of these Guidelines should include specific materiality thresholds that take into account the size and the nature of the local economy, the importance of the MNE group in that economy, and the size and nature of local operating entities, in addition to the overall size and nature of the MNE group. Measures of materiality may be considered in relative terms (e.g. transactions not exceeding a percentage of revenue or a percentage of cost measure) or in absolute amount terms (e.g. transactions not exceeding a certain fixed amount). Individual countries should establish their own materiality standards for local file purposes, based on local conditions. The materiality standards should be objective standards that are commonly understood and accepted in commercial practice. See paragraph 18 for the materiality standards applicable in completing the master file.

33. A number of countries have introduced in their transfer pricing documentation rules simplification measures which exempt small and medium-sized enterprises (SMEs) from transfer pricing documentation requirements or limit the information required to be provided by such enterprises. In order not to impose on taxpayers costs and burdens disproportionate to the circumstances, it is recommended to not require SMEs to produce the amount of documentation that might be expected from larger enterprises. However, SMEs should be obliged to provide information and documents about their material cross-border transactions upon a specific request of the tax administration in the course of a tax examination or for transfer pricing risk assessment purposes.

34. For purposes of Annex III to Chapter V of these Guidelines, the Country-by-Country Report should include all tax jurisdictions in which the MNE group has an entity resident for tax purposes, regardless of the size of business operations in that tax jurisdiction.

D.4. Retention of documents

35. Taxpayers should not be obliged to retain documents beyond a reasonable period consistent with the requirements of domestic law at either the parent company or local entity level. However, at times materials and information required in the documentation package (master file, local file and Country-by-Country Report) may be relevant to a transfer pricing enquiry for a subsequent year that is not time barred, for example where taxpayers voluntarily keep such records in relation to long-term contracts, or to determine whether comparability standards relating to the application of a transfer pricing method in that subsequent year are satisfied. Tax administrations should bear in mind the difficulties in locating documents for prior years and should restrict such requests to instances where they have good reason in connection with the transaction under examination for reviewing the documents in question.

36. Because the tax administration's ultimate interest would be satisfied if the necessary documents were submitted in a timely manner when requested by the tax administration in the course of an examination, the way that documentation is stored – whether in paper, electronic form, or in any other system – should be at the discretion of the taxpayer provided that relevant information can promptly be made available to the tax administration in the form specified by the local country rules and practices.

D.5. Frequency of documentation updates

37. It is recommended that transfer pricing documentation be periodically reviewed in order to determine whether functional and economic analyses are still accurate and relevant and to confirm the validity of the applied transfer pricing methodology. In general, the master file, the local file and the Country-by-Country Report should be reviewed and updated annually. It is recognised, however, that in many situations business descriptions, functional analyses, and descriptions of comparables may not change significantly from year to year.

38. In order to simplify compliance burdens on taxpayers, tax administrations may determine, as long as the operating conditions remain unchanged, that the searches in databases for comparables supporting part of the local file be updated every three years rather than annually. Financial data for the comparables should nonetheless be updated every year in order to apply the arm's length principle reliably.

D.6. Language

39. The necessity of providing documentation in local language may constitute a complicating factor with respect to transfer pricing compliance to the extent that substantial time and cost may be involved in translating documents. The language in which transfer pricing documentation should be submitted should be established under local laws. Countries are encouraged to permit filing of transfer pricing documentation in commonly used languages where it will not compromise the usefulness of the documents. Where tax administrations believe that translation of documents is necessary, they should make specific requests for translation and provide sufficient time to make such translation as comfortable a burden as possible.

D.7. Penalties

40. Many countries have adopted documentation-related penalties to ensure efficient operation of transfer pricing documentation requirements. They are designed to make non-compliance more costly than compliance. Penalty regimes are governed by the laws of each individual country. Country practices with regard to transfer pricing documentation-related penalties vary widely. The existence of different local country penalty regimes may influence the quality of taxpayers' compliance so that taxpayers could be driven to favour one country over another in their compliance practices.

41. Documentation-related penalties imposed for failure to comply with transfer pricing documentation requirements or failure to timely submit required information are usually civil (or administrative) monetary penalties. These documentation-related penalties are based on a fixed amount that may be assessed for each document missing or for each fiscal year under review, or calculated as a percentage of the related tax understatement ultimately determined, a percentage of the related adjustment to the income, or as a percentage of the amount of the cross-border transactions not documented.

42. Care should be taken not to impose a documentation-related penalty on a taxpayer for failing to submit data to which the MNE group did not have access. However, a decision not to impose documentation-related penalties does not mean that adjustments cannot be made to income where prices are not consistent with the arm's length principle. The fact that positions are fully documented does not necessarily mean that the taxpayer's positions are correct. Moreover, an assertion by a local entity that other group members are responsible for transfer pricing compliance is not a sufficient reason for that entity to fail to provide required documentation, nor should such an assertion prevent the imposition of documentation-related penalties for failure to comply with documentation rules where the necessary information is not forthcoming.

43. Another way for countries to encourage taxpayers to fulfil transfer pricing documentation requirements is by designing compliance incentives such as penalty protection or a shift in the burden of proof. Where the documentation meets the requirements and is timely submitted, the taxpayer could be exempted from tax penalties or subject to a lower penalty rate if a transfer pricing adjustment is made and sustained, notwithstanding the provision of documentation. In some jurisdictions where the taxpayer bears the burden of proof regarding transfer pricing matters, a shift of the burden of proof to the tax administration's side where adequate documentation is provided on a timely basis offers another measure that could be used to create an incentive for transfer pricing documentation compliance.

D.8. Confidentiality

44. Tax administrations should take all reasonable steps to ensure that there is no public disclosure of confidential information (trade secrets, scientific secrets, etc.) and other commercially sensitive information contained in the documentation package (master file, local file and Country-by-Country Report). Tax administrations should also assure taxpayers that the information presented in transfer pricing documentation will remain confidential. In cases where disclosure is required in public court proceedings or judicial decisions, every effort should be made to ensure that confidentiality is maintained and that information is disclosed only to the extent needed.

45. The OECD Guide (2012) "Keeping It Safe" on the protection of confidentiality of information exchanged for tax purposes provides guidance on the rules and practices that

must be in place to ensure the confidentiality of tax information exchanged under exchange of information instruments.

D.9. Other issues

46. The requirement to use the most reliable information will usually, but not always, require the use of local comparables over the use of regional comparables where such local comparables are reasonably available. The use of regional comparables in transfer pricing documentation prepared for countries in the same geographic region in situations where appropriate local comparables are available will not, in some cases, comport with the obligation to rely on the most reliable information. While the simplification benefits of limiting the number of comparable searches a company is required to undertake are obvious, and materiality and compliance costs are relevant factors to consider, a desire for simplifying compliance processes should not go so far as to undermine compliance with the requirement to use the most reliable available information. See paragraphs 1.57-1.58 on market differences and multi-country analyses for further detail of when local comparables are to be preferred.

47. It is not recommended, particularly at the stage of transfer pricing risk assessment, to require that the transfer pricing documentation should be certified by an outside auditor or other third party. Similarly, mandatory use of consulting firms to prepare transfer pricing documentation is not recommended.

E. Implementation

48. It is essential that the guidance in this chapter, and in particular the Country-by-Country Report, be implemented effectively and consistently. Therefore, countries participating in the OECD/G20 Base Erosion and Profit Shifting (BEPS) Project have developed the following guidance on implementation of transfer pricing documentation and Country-by-Country Reporting.

E.1. Master file and Local file

49. It is recommended that the master file and local file elements of the transfer pricing documentation standard be implemented through local country legislation or administrative procedures and that the master file and local file be filed directly with the tax administrations in each relevant jurisdiction as required by those administrations. Countries participating in the OECD/G20 BEPS Project agree that with regard to the local file and the master file confidentiality and consistent use of the standards contained in Annex I and Annex II of Chapter V of these Guidelines should be taken into account when introducing these elements in local country legislation or administrative procedures.

E.2. Country-by-Country Report

E.2.1. Timing: When should the Country-by-Country Reporting requirement start?

50. It is recommended that the first Country-by-Country Reports be required to be filed for MNE fiscal years beginning on or after 1 January 2016. However, it is acknowledged that some jurisdictions may need time to follow their particular domestic legislative process in order to make necessary adjustments to the law. In order to assist countries in preparing timely legislation, model legislation requiring ultimate parent entities of MNE

groups to file the Country-by-Country Report in their jurisdiction of residence has been developed (see Annex IV to Chapter V of these Guidelines). Jurisdictions will be able to adapt this model legislation to their own legal systems. Given the recommendation in paragraph 31 that MNEs be allowed one year from the close of the fiscal year to which the Country-by-Country Report relates to prepare and file the Country-by-Country Report, this recommendation means that the first Country-by-Country Reports would be filed by 31 December 2017. For MNEs with a fiscal year ending on a date other than 31 December, the first Country-by-Country Reports would be required to be filed later in 2018, twelve months after the close of the relevant MNE fiscal year, and would report on the MNE group's first fiscal year beginning after 1 January 2016. It follows from this recommendation that the countries participating in the OECD/G20 BEPS Project agree that they will not require filing of a Country-by-Country Report based on the new template for MNE fiscal years beginning prior to 1 January 2016. The MNE fiscal year relates to the consolidated reporting period for financial statement purposes and not to taxable years or to the financial reporting periods of individual subsidiaries.

E.2.2. Which MNE groups should be required to file the Country-by-Country Report?

51. It is recommended that all MNE groups be required to file the Country-by-Country Report each year except as follows.

52. There would be an exemption from the general filing requirement for MNE groups with annual consolidated group revenue in the immediately preceding fiscal year of less than EUR 750 million or a near equivalent amount in domestic currency as of January 2015. Thus, for example, if an MNE that keeps its financial accounts on a calendar year basis has EUR 625 million in consolidated group revenue for its 2015 calendar year, it would not be required to file the Country-by-Country Report in any country with respect to its fiscal year ending 31 December 2016.

53. It is believed that the exemption described in paragraph 52, which provides a threshold of EUR 750 million, will exclude approximately 85 to 90 percent of MNE groups from the requirement to file the Country-by-Country Report, but that the Country-by-Country Report will nevertheless be filed by MNE groups controlling approximately 90 percent of corporate revenues. The prescribed exemption threshold therefore represents an appropriate balancing of reporting burden and benefit to tax administrations.

54. It is the intention of the countries participating in the OECD/G20 BEPS Project to reconsider the appropriateness of the applicable revenue threshold described in the preceding paragraph in connection with their 2020 review of implementation of the new standard, including whether additional or different data should be reported.

55. It is considered that no exemptions from filing the Country-by-Country Report should be adopted apart from the exemptions outlined in this section. In particular, no special industry exemptions should be provided, no general exemption for investment funds should be provided, and no exemption for non-corporate entities or non-public corporate entities should be provided. Notwithstanding this conclusion, countries participating in the OECD/G20 BEPS Project agree that MNE groups with income derived from international transportation or transportation in inland waterways that is covered by treaty provisions that are specific to such income and under which the taxing rights on such income are allocated exclusively to one jurisdiction, should include the information required by the country-by-country template with respect to such income only against the name of the jurisdiction to which the relevant treaty provisions allocate these taxing rights.

E.2.3. Necessary conditions underpinning the obtaining and the use of the Country-by-Country Report

56. Countries participating in the OECD/G20 BEPS Project agree to the following conditions underpinning the obtaining and the use of the Country-by-Country Report.

Confidentiality

57. Jurisdictions should have in place and enforce legal protections of the confidentiality of the reported information. Such protections would preserve the confidentiality of the Country-by-Country Report to an extent at least equivalent to the protections that would apply if such information were delivered to the country under the provisions of the Multilateral Convention on Mutual Administrative Assistance in Tax Matters, a Tax Information Exchange Agreement (TIEA) or a tax treaty that meets the internationally agreed standard of information upon request as reviewed by the Global Forum on Transparency and Exchange of Information for Tax Purposes. Such protections include limitation of the use of information, rules on the persons to whom the information may be disclosed, ordre public, etc.

Consistency

58. Jurisdictions should use their best efforts to adopt a legal requirement that MNE groups' ultimate parent entities resident in their jurisdiction prepare and file the Country-by-Country Report, unless exempted as set out in paragraph 52. Jurisdictions should utilise the standard template contained in Annex III of Chapter V of these Guidelines. Stated otherwise, under this condition no jurisdiction will require that the Country-by-Country Report contain either additional information not contained in Annex III, nor will it fail to require reporting of information included in Annex III.

Appropriate Use

59. Jurisdictions should use appropriately the information in the Country-by-Country Report template in accordance with paragraph 25. In particular, jurisdictions will commit to use the Country-by-Country Report for assessing high-level transfer pricing risk. Jurisdictions may also use the Country-by-Country Report for assessing other BEPS-related risks. Jurisdictions should not propose adjustments to the income of any taxpayer on the basis of an income allocation formula based on the data from the Country-by-Country Report. They will further commit that if such adjustments based on Country-by-Country Report data are made by the local tax administration of the jurisdiction, the jurisdiction's competent authority will promptly concede the adjustment in any relevant competent authority proceeding. This does not imply, however, that jurisdictions would be prevented from using the Country-by-Country Report data as a basis for making further enquiries into the MNE's transfer pricing arrangements or into other tax matters in the course of a tax audit.[1]

E.2.4. The framework for government-to-government mechanisms to exchange Country-by-Country Reports and implementation package

E.2.4.1. Framework

60. Jurisdictions should require in a timely manner Country-by-Country Reporting from ultimate parent entities of MNE groups resident in their country and referred to in Section E.2.2 and exchange this information on an automatic basis with the jurisdictions in which the MNE group operates and which fulfil the conditions listed in Section E.2.3. In case a jurisdiction fails to provide information to a jurisdiction fulfilling the conditions listed in Section E.2.3, because (a) it has not required Country-by-Country Reporting from the ultimate parent entity of such MNE groups, (b) no competent authority agreement has been agreed in a timely manner under the current international agreements of the jurisdiction for the exchange of the Country-by-Country Reports or (c) it has been established that there is a failure to exchange the information in practice with a jurisdiction after agreeing with that jurisdiction to do so, a secondary mechanism would be accepted as appropriate, through local filing or through filing of the Country-by-Country Reports by a designated member of the MNE group acting in place of the ultimate parent entity and automatic exchange of these reports by its country of tax residence.

E.2.4.2. Implementation Package

61. Countries participating in the OECD/G20 BEPS Project have therefore developed an implementation package for government-to-government exchange of Country-by-Country Reports contained in Annex IV to Chapter V of these Guidelines.

More specifically:

- Model legislation requiring the ultimate parent entity of an MNE group to file the Country-by-Country Report in its jurisdiction of residence has been developed. Jurisdictions will be able to adapt this model legislation to their own legal systems, where changes to current legislation are required. Key elements of secondary mechanisms have also been developed.
- Implementing arrangements for the automatic exchange of the Country-by-Country Reports under international agreements have been developed, incorporating the conditions set out in Section E.2.3. Such implementing arrangements include competent authority agreements ("CAAs") based on existing international agreements (the Multilateral Convention on Mutual Administrative Assistance in Tax Matters, bilateral tax treaties and TIEAs) and inspired by the existing models developed by the OECD working with G20 countries for the automatic exchange of financial account information.

62. Participating jurisdictions endeavour to introduce as necessary domestic legislation in a timely manner. They are also encouraged to expand the coverage of their international agreements for exchange of information. The implementation of the package will be monitored on an ongoing basis. The outcomes of this monitoring will be taken into consideration in the 2020 review.

Note

1. Access to a mutual agreement procedure (MAP) will be available when the government-to-government exchange of the Country-by-Country Reports is based on bilateral treaties. In cases where the international agreements on which the government-to-government exchanges of the Country-by-Country Reports are based do not contain provisions providing access to MAP, countries commit to introducing in the competent authority agreement to be developed a mechanism for competent authority procedures to discuss with the aim of resolving cases of undesirable economic outcomes, including if such cases arise for individual businesses.

Annex I to Chapter V

Transfer pricing documentation – Master file

The following information should be included in the master file:

Organisational structure

- Chart illustrating the MNE's legal and ownership structure and geographical location of operating entities.

Description of MNE's business(es)

- General written description of the MNE's business including:
  - Important drivers of business profit;
  - A description of the supply chain for the group's five largest products and/or service offerings by turnover plus any other products and/or services amounting to more than 5 percent of group turnover. The required description could take the form of a chart or a diagram;
  - A list and brief description of important service arrangements between members of the MNE group, other than research and development (R&D) services, including a description of the capabilities of the principal locations providing important services and transfer pricing policies for allocating services costs and determining prices to be paid for intra-group services;
  - A description of the main geographic markets for the group's products and services that are referred to in the second bullet point above;
  - A brief written functional analysis describing the principal contributions to value creation by individual entities within the group, i.e. key functions performed, important risks assumed, and important assets used;
  - A description of important business restructuring transactions, acquisitions and divestitures occurring during the fiscal year.

MNE's intangibles (as defined in Chapter VI of these Guidelines)

- A general description of the MNE's overall strategy for the development, ownership and exploitation of intangibles, including location of principal R&D facilities and location of R&D management.

- A list of intangibles or groups of intangibles of the MNE group that are important for transfer pricing purposes and which entities legally own them.
- A list of important agreements among identified associated enterprises related to intangibles, including cost contribution arrangements, principal research service agreements and licence agreements.
- A general description of the group's transfer pricing policies related to R&D and intangibles.
- A general description of any important transfers of interests in intangibles among associated enterprises during the fiscal year concerned, including the entities, countries, and compensation involved.

MNE's intercompany financial activities

- A general description of how the group is financed, including important financing arrangements with unrelated lenders.
- The identification of any members of the MNE group that provide a central financing function for the group, including the country under whose laws the entity is organised and the place of effective management of such entities.
- A general description of the MNE's general transfer pricing policies related to financing arrangements between associated enterprises.

MNE's financial and tax positions

- The MNE's annual consolidated financial statement for the fiscal year concerned if otherwise prepared for financial reporting, regulatory, internal management, tax or other purposes.
- A list and brief description of the MNE group's existing unilateral advance pricing agreements (APAs) and other tax rulings relating to the allocation of income among countries.

Annex II to Chapter V

Transfer pricing documentation – Local file

The following information should be included in the local file:

Local entity

- A description of the management structure of the local entity, a local organisation chart, and a description of the individuals to whom local management reports and the country(ies) in which such individuals maintain their principal offices.
- A detailed description of the business and business strategy pursued by the local entity including an indication whether the local entity has been involved in or affected by business restructurings or intangibles transfers in the present or immediately past year and an explanation of those aspects of such transactions affecting the local entity.
- Key competitors.

Controlled transactions

For each material category of controlled transactions in which the entity is involved, provide the following information:

- A description of the material controlled transactions (e.g. procurement of manufacturing services, purchase of goods, provision of services, loans, financial and performance guarantees, licences of intangibles, etc.) and the context in which such transactions take place.
- The amount of intra-group payments and receipts for each category of controlled transactions involving the local entity (i.e. payments and receipts for products, services, royalties, interest, etc.) broken down by tax jurisdiction of the foreign payor or recipient.
- An identification of associated enterprises involved in each category of controlled transactions, and the relationship amongst them.
- Copies of all material intercompany agreements concluded by the local entity.
- A detailed comparability and functional analysis of the taxpayer and relevant associated enterprises with respect to each documented category of controlled transactions, including any changes compared to prior years.[1]
- An indication of the most appropriate transfer pricing method with regard to the category of transaction and the reasons for selecting that method.

- An indication of which associated enterprise is selected as the tested party, if applicable, and an explanation of the reasons for this selection.
- A summary of the important assumptions made in applying the transfer pricing methodology.
- If relevant, an explanation of the reasons for performing a multi-year analysis.
- A list and description of selected comparable uncontrolled transactions (internal or external), if any, and information on relevant financial indicators for independent enterprises relied on in the transfer pricing analysis, including a description of the comparable search methodology and the source of such information.
- A description of any comparability adjustments performed, and an indication of whether adjustments have been made to the results of the tested party, the comparable uncontrolled transactions, or both.
- A description of the reasons for concluding that relevant transactions were priced on an arm's length basis based on the application of the selected transfer pricing method.
- A summary of financial information used in applying the transfer pricing methodology.
- A copy of existing unilateral and bilateral/multilateral APAs and other tax rulings to which the local tax jurisdiction is not a party and which are related to controlled transactions described above.

Financial information

- Annual local entity financial accounts for the fiscal year concerned. If audited statements exist they should be supplied and if not, existing unaudited statements should be supplied.
- Information and allocation schedules showing how the financial data used in applying the transfer pricing method may be tied to the annual financial statements.
- Summary schedules of relevant financial data for comparables used in the analysis and the sources from which that data was obtained.

Note

1. To the extent this functional analysis duplicates information in the master file, a cross-reference to the master file is sufficient.

Annex III to Chapter V

Transfer pricing documentation – Country-by-Country Report

A. Model template for the Country-by-Country Report

Table 1. **Overview of allocation of income, taxes and business activities by tax jurisdiction**

Name of the MNE group: Fiscal year concerned: Currency used:										
Tax Jurisdiction	Revenues			Profit (Loss) before Income Tax	Income Tax Paid (on Cash Basis)	Income Tax Accrued – Current Year	Stated Capital	Accumulated Earnings	Number of Employees	Tangible Assets other than Cash and Cash Equivalents
	Unrelated Party	Related Party	Total							

Table 2. **List of all the Constituent Entities of the MNE group included in each aggregation per tax jurisdiction**

Name of the MNE group: Fiscal year concerned:															
Tax Jurisdiction	Constituent Entities Resident in the Tax Jurisdiction	Tax Jurisdiction of Organisation or Incorporation if Different from Tax Jurisdiction of Residence	Main Business Activity(ies)												
			Research and Development	Holding or Managing Intellectual Property	Purchasing or Procurement	Manufacturing or Production	Sales, Marketing or Distribution	Administrative, Management or Support Services	Provision of Services to Unrelated Parties	Internal Group Finance	Regulated Financial Services	Insurance	Holding Shares or Other Equity instruments	Dormant	Other[1]
	1.														
	2.														
	3.														
	1.														
	2.														
	3.														

1. Please specify the nature of the activity of the Constituent Entity in the "Additional Information" section.

Table 3. **Additional Information**

Name of the MNE group: Fiscal year concerned:
Please include any further brief information or explanation you consider necessary or that would facilitate the understanding of the compulsory information provided in the Country-by-Country Report.

B. Template for the Country-by-Country Report – General instructions

Purpose

This Annex III to Chapter V of these Guidelines contains a template for reporting a multinational enterprise's (MNE) group allocation of income, taxes and business activities on a tax jurisdiction-by-tax jurisdiction basis. These instructions form an integral part of the model template for the Country-by-Country Report.

Definitions

Reporting MNE

A Reporting MNE is the ultimate parent entity of an MNE group.

Constituent Entity

For purposes of completing Annex III, a Constituent Entity of the MNE group is (i) any separate business unit of an MNE group that is included in the Consolidated Financial Statements of the MNE group for financial reporting purposes, or would be so included if equity interests in such business unit of the MNE group were traded on a public securities exchange; (ii) any such business unit that is excluded from the MNE group's Consolidated Financial Statements solely on size or materiality grounds; and (iii) any permanent establishment of any separate business unit of the MNE group included in (i) or (ii) above provided the business unit prepares a separate financial statement for such permanent establishment for financial reporting, regulatory, tax reporting, or internal management control purposes.

Treatment of Branches and Permanent Establishments

The permanent establishment data should be reported by reference to the tax jurisdiction in which it is situated and not by reference to the tax jurisdiction of residence of the business unit of which the permanent establishment is a part. Residence tax jurisdiction reporting for the business unit of which the permanent establishment is a part should exclude financial data related to the permanent establishment.

Consolidated Financial Statements

The Consolidated Financial Statements are the financial statements of an MNE group in which the assets, liabilities, income, expenses and cash flows of the ultimate parent entity and the Constituent Entities are presented as those of a single economic entity.

Period covered by the annual template

The template should cover the fiscal year of the Reporting MNE. For Constituent Entities, at the discretion of the Reporting MNE, the template should reflect on a consistent basis either (i) information for the fiscal year of the relevant Constituent Entities ending on the same date as the fiscal year of the Reporting MNE, or ending within the 12 month period preceding such date, or (ii) information for all the relevant Constituent Entities reported for the fiscal year of the Reporting MNE.

Source of data

The Reporting MNE should consistently use the same sources of data from year to year in completing the template. The Reporting MNE may choose to use data from its consolidation reporting packages, from separate entity statutory financial statements, regulatory financial statements, or internal management accounts. It is not necessary to reconcile the revenue, profit and tax reporting in the template to the consolidated financial statements. If statutory financial statements are used as the basis for reporting, all amounts should be translated to the stated functional currency of the Reporting MNE at the average exchange rate for the year stated in the Additional Information section of the template. Adjustments need not be made, however, for differences in accounting principles applied from tax jurisdiction to tax jurisdiction.

The Reporting MNE should provide a brief description of the sources of data used in preparing the template in the Additional Information section of the template. If a change is made in the source of data used from year to year, the Reporting MNE should explain the reasons for the change and its consequences in the Additional Information section of the template.

C. Template for the Country-by-Country Report – Specific instructions

Overview of allocation of income, taxes and business activities by tax jurisdiction (Table 1)

Tax Jurisdiction

In the first column of the template, the Reporting MNE should list all of the tax jurisdictions in which Constituent Entities of the MNE group are resident for tax purposes. A tax jurisdiction is defined as a State as well as a non-State jurisdiction which has fiscal autonomy. A separate line should be included for all Constituent Entities in the MNE group deemed by the Reporting MNE not to be resident in any tax jurisdiction for tax purposes. Where a Constituent Entity is resident in more than one tax jurisdiction, the applicable tax treaty tie breaker should be applied to determine the tax jurisdiction of residence. Where no applicable tax treaty exists, the Constituent Entity should be reported in the tax jurisdiction of the Constituent Entity's place of effective management. The place of effective management should be determined in accordance with the provisions of Article 4 of the OECD Model Tax Convention and its accompanying Commentary.

Revenues

In the three columns of the template under the heading Revenues, the Reporting MNE should report the following information: (i) the sum of revenues of all the Constituent Entities of the MNE group in the relevant tax jurisdiction generated from transactions with associated enterprises; (ii) the sum of revenues of all the Constituent Entities of the MNE group in the relevant tax jurisdiction generated from transactions with independent parties; and (iii) the total of (i) and (ii). Revenues should include revenues from sales of inventory and properties, services, royalties, interest, premiums and any other amounts. Revenues should exclude payments received from other Constituent Entities that are treated as dividends in the payor's tax jurisdiction.

Profit (Loss) before Income Tax

In the fifth column of the template, the Reporting MNE should report the sum of the profit (loss) before income tax for all the Constituent Entities resident for tax purposes in the relevant tax jurisdiction. The profit (loss) before income tax should include all extraordinary income and expense items.

Income Tax Paid (on Cash Basis)

In the sixth column of the template, the Reporting MNE should report the total amount of income tax actually paid during the relevant fiscal year by all the Constituent Entities resident for tax purposes in the relevant tax jurisdiction. Taxes paid should include cash taxes paid by the Constituent Entity to the residence tax jurisdiction and to all other tax jurisdictions. Taxes paid should include withholding taxes paid by other entities (associated enterprises and independent enterprises) with respect to payments to the Constituent Entity. Thus, if company A resident in tax jurisdiction A earns interest in tax jurisdiction B, the tax withheld in tax jurisdiction B should be reported by company A.

Income Tax Accrued (Current Year)

In the seventh column of the template, the Reporting MNE should report the sum of the accrued current tax expense recorded on taxable profits or losses of the year of reporting of all the Constituent Entities resident for tax purposes in the relevant tax jurisdiction. The current tax expense should reflect only operations in the current year and should not include deferred taxes or provisions for uncertain tax liabilities.

Stated Capital

In the eighth column of the template, the Reporting MNE should report the sum of the stated capital of all the Constituent Entities resident for tax purposes in the relevant tax jurisdiction. With regard to permanent establishments, the stated capital should be reported by the legal entity of which it is a permanent establishment unless there is a defined capital requirement in the permanent establishment tax jurisdiction for regulatory purposes.

Accumulated Earnings

In the ninth column of the template, the Reporting MNE should report the sum of the total accumulated earnings of all the Constituent Entities resident for tax purposes in the relevant tax jurisdiction as of the end of the year. With regard to permanent establishments, accumulated earnings should be reported by the legal entity of which it is a permanent establishment.

Number of Employees

In the tenth column of the template, the Reporting MNE should report the total number of employees on a full-time equivalent (FTE) basis of all the Constituent Entities resident for tax purposes in the relevant tax jurisdiction. The number of employees may be reported as of the year-end, on the basis of average employment levels for the year, or on any other basis consistently applied across tax jurisdictions and from year to year. For this purpose, independent contractors participating in the ordinary operating activities of the Constituent Entity may be reported as employees. Reasonable rounding or approximation of the number of employees is permissible, providing that such rounding or approximation does not materially distort the relative distribution of employees across the various tax jurisdictions. Consistent approaches should be applied from year to year and across entities.

Tangible Assets other than Cash and Cash Equivalents

In the eleventh column of the template, the Reporting MNE should report the sum of the net book values of tangible assets of all the Constituent Entities resident for tax purposes in the relevant tax jurisdiction. With regard to permanent establishments, assets should be reported by reference to the tax jurisdiction in which the permanent establishment is situated. Tangible assets for this purpose do not include cash or cash equivalents, intangibles, or financial assets.

List of all the Constituent Entities of the MNE group included in each aggregation per tax jurisdiction (Table 2)

Constituent Entities Resident in the Tax Jurisdiction

The Reporting MNE should list, on a tax jurisdiction-by-tax jurisdiction basis and by legal entity name, all the Constituent Entities of the MNE group which are resident for tax purposes in the relevant tax jurisdiction. As stated above with regard to permanent establishments, however, the permanent establishment should be listed by reference to the tax jurisdiction in which it is situated. The legal entity of which it is a permanent establishment should be noted (e.g. XYZ Corp – Tax Jurisdiction A PE).

Tax Jurisdiction of Organisation or Incorporation if Different from Tax Jurisdiction of Residence

The Reporting MNE should report the name of the tax jurisdiction under whose laws the Constituent Entity of the MNE is organised or incorporated if it is different from the tax jurisdiction of residence.

Main Business Activity(ies)

The Reporting MNE should determine the nature of the main business activity(ies) carried out by the Constituent Entity in the relevant tax jurisdiction, by ticking one or more of the appropriate boxes.

Business Activities
Research and Development
Holding or Managing Intellectual Property
Purchasing or Procurement
Manufacturing or Production
Sales, Marketing or Distribution
Administrative, Management or Support Services
Provision of Services to Unrelated Parties
Internal Group Finance
Regulated Financial Services
Insurance
Holding Shares or Other Equity Instruments
Dormant
Other[1]

1. Please specify the nature of the activity of the Constituent Entity in the "Additional Information" section.

Annex IV to Chapter V

Country-by-Country Reporting Implementation Package

Introduction

In order to facilitate a consistent and swift implementation of the Country-by-Country Reporting developed under Action 13 of the Base Erosion and Profit Shifting Action Plan (BEPS Action Plan, OECD, 2013), a Country-by-Country Reporting Implementation Package has been agreed by countries participating in the OECD/G20 BEPS Project. This implementation package consists of (i) model legislation which could be used by countries to require the ultimate parent entity of an MNE group to file the Country-by-Country Report in its jurisdiction of residence including backup filing requirements and (ii) three model Competent Authority Agreements that are to be used to facilitate implementation of the exchange of Country-by-Country Reports, respectively based on the 1) Convention on Mutual Administrative Assistance in Tax Matters, 2) bilateral tax conventions and 3) Tax Information Exchange Agreements (TIEAs). It is recognised that developing countries may require support for the effective implementation of Country-by-Country Reporting.

Model legislation

The model legislation contained in the Country-by-Country Reporting Implementation Package takes into account neither the constitutional law and legal system, nor the structure and wording of the tax legislation of any particular jurisdiction. Jurisdictions will be able to adapt this model legislation to their own legal systems, where changes to current legislation are required.

Competent Authority Agreements

The Convention on Mutual Administrative Assistance in Tax Matters (the "Convention'), by virtue of its Article 6, requires the Competent Authorities of the Parties to the Convention to mutually agree on the scope of the automatic exchange of information and the procedure to be complied with. In the context of the Common Reporting Standard, this requirement has been translated into a Multilateral Competent Authority Agreement, which defines the scope, timing, procedures and safeguards according to which the automatic exchange should take place.

As the implementation of the automatic exchange of information by means of a Multilateral Competent Authority Agreement in the context of the Common Reporting Standard has proven both time- and resource-efficient, the same approach could be used for the purpose of putting the automatic exchange of information in relation to Country-by-Country Reports in place. Therefore, the Multilateral Competent Authority Agreement on the Exchange of Country-by-Country Reports (the "CbC MCAA") has been developed, based on the Convention and inspired by the Multilateral Competent Authority Agreement concluded in the context of the implementation of the Common Reporting Standard. In addition, two further model competent authority agreements have been developed for exchanges of Country-by-Country Reports, one for exchanges under Double Tax Conventions and one for exchanges under Tax Information Exchange Agreements.

In line with paragraph 5 of Chapter V of these Guidelines, one of the three objectives of transfer pricing documentation is to provide tax administrations with the information necessary to conduct an informed transfer pricing risk assessment, while paragraph 10 of Chapter V of these Guidelines states that effective risk identification and assessment constitute an essential early stage in the process of selecting appropriate cases for transfer pricing audit. The Country-by-Country Reports exchanged on the basis of the model competent authority agreements contained in the present Country-by-Country Reporting Implementation Package, represent one of the three tiers of the transfer pricing documentation and will, in accordance with paragraphs 16, 17 and 25 of Chapter V of these Guidelines, provide tax administrations with relevant and reliable information to perform an efficient and robust transfer pricing risk assessment analysis. Against that background, the model competent authority agreements aim to provide the framework to make the information contained in the Country-by-Country Report available to concerned tax authorities, such information being foreseeably relevant for the administration and enforcement of their tax laws through the automatic exchange of information.

The purpose of the CbC MCAA is to set forth rules and procedures as may be necessary for Competent Authorities of jurisdictions implementing BEPS Action 13 to automatically exchange Country-by-Country Reports prepared by the Reporting Entity of an MNE Group and filed on an annual basis with the tax authorities of the jurisdiction of tax residence of that entity with the tax authorities of all jurisdictions in which the MNE Group operates.

For most provisions, the wording is substantially the same as the text of the Multilateral Competent Authority Agreement for the purpose of exchanges under the Common Reporting Standard. Where appropriate, the wording has been complemented or amended to reflect the Guidance on Country-by-Country Reporting set out in Chapter V of these Guidelines.

As a next step, it is intended that an XML Schema and a related User Guide will be developed with a view to accommodating the electronic exchange of Country-by-Country Reports.

Model legislation related to Country-by-Country Reporting

Article 1
Definitions

For purposes of this [title of the law] the following terms have the following meanings:

1. The term "Group" means a collection of enterprises related through ownership or control such that it is either required to prepare Consolidated Financial Statements for financial reporting purposes under applicable accounting principles or would be so required if equity interests in any of the enterprises were traded on a public securities exchange.

2. The term "MNE Group" means any Group that (i) includes two or more enterprises the tax residence for which is in different jurisdictions, or includes an enterprise that is resident for tax purposes in one jurisdiction and is subject to tax with respect to the business carried out through a permanent establishment in another jurisdiction, and (ii) is not an Excluded MNE Group.

3. The term "Excluded MNE Group" means, with respect to any Fiscal Year of the Group, a Group having total consolidated group revenue of less than [750 million Euro]/ [insert an amount in local currency approximately equivalent to 750 million Euro as of January 2015] during the Fiscal Year immediately preceding the Reporting Fiscal Year as reflected in its Consolidated Financial Statements for such preceding Fiscal Year.

4. The term "Constituent Entity" means (i) any separate business unit of an MNE Group that is included in the Consolidated Financial Statements of the MNE Group for financial reporting purposes, or would be so included if equity interests in such business unit of an MNE Group were traded on a public securities exchange; (ii) any such business unit that is excluded from the MNE Group's Consolidated Financial Statements solely on size or materiality grounds; and (iii) any permanent establishment of any separate business unit of the MNE Group included in (i) or (ii) above provided the business unit prepares a separate financial statement for such permanent establishment for financial reporting, regulatory, tax reporting, or internal management control purposes.

5. The term "Reporting Entity" means the Constituent Entity that is required to file a country-by-report conforming to the requirements in Article 4 in its jurisdiction of tax residence on behalf of the MNE Group. The Reporting Entity may be the Ultimate Parent Entity, the Surrogate Parent Entity, or any entity described in paragraph 2 of Article 2.

6. The term "Ultimate Parent Entity" means a Constituent Entity of an MNE Group that meets the following criteria:

(i) it owns directly or indirectly a sufficient interest in one or more other Constituent Entities of such MNE Group such that it is required to prepare Consolidated Financial Statements under accounting principles generally applied in its jurisdiction of tax residence, or would be so required if its equity interests were traded on a public securities exchange in its jurisdiction of tax residence; and

(ii) there is no other Constituent Entity of such MNE Group that owns directly or indirectly an interest described in subsection (i) above in the first mentioned Constituent Entity.

7. The term "Surrogate Parent Entity" means one Constituent Entity of the MNE Group that has been appointed by such MNE Group, as a sole substitute for the Ultimate Parent Entity, to file the Country-by-Country Report in that Constituent Entity's jurisdiction of tax residence, on behalf of such MNE Group, when one or more of the conditions set out in subsection (ii) of paragraph 2 of Article 2 applies.

8. The term "Fiscal Year" means an annual accounting period with respect to which the Ultimate Parent Entity of the MNE Group prepares its financial statements.

9. The term "Reporting Fiscal Year" means that Fiscal Year the financial and operational results of which are reflected in the Country-by-Country Report defined in Article 4.

10. The term "Qualifying Competent Authority Agreement" means an agreement (i) that is between authorised representatives of those jurisdictions that are parties to an International Agreement and (ii) that requires the automatic exchange of Country-by-Country Reports between the party jurisdictions.

11. The term "International Agreement" shall mean the Multilateral Convention for Mutual Administrative Assistance in Tax Matters, any bilateral or multilateral Tax Convention, or any Tax Information Exchange Agreement to which [Country] is a party, and that by its terms provides legal authority for the exchange of tax information between jurisdictions, including automatic exchange of such information.

12. The term "Consolidated Financial Statements" means the financial statements of an MNE Group in which the assets, liabilities, income, expenses and cash flows of the Ultimate Parent Entity and the Constituent Entities are presented as those of a single economic entity.

13. The term "Systemic Failure" with respect to a jurisdiction means that a jurisdiction has a Qualifying Competent Authority Agreement in effect with [Country], but has suspended automatic exchange (for reasons other than those that are in accordance with the terms of that Agreement) or otherwise persistently failed to automatically provide to [Country] Country-by-Country Reports in its possession of MNE Groups that have Constituent Entities in [Country].

Article 2
Filing Obligation

1. Each Ultimate Parent Entity of an MNE Group that is resident for tax purposes in [Country] shall file a Country-by-Country Report conforming to the requirements of Article 4 with the [Country Tax Administration] with respect to its Reporting Fiscal Year on or before the date specified in Article 5.

2. A Constituent Entity which is not the Ultimate Parent Entity of an MNE Group shall file a Country-by-Country Report conforming to the requirements of Article 4 with the [Country Tax Administration] with respect to the Reporting Fiscal Year of an MNE Group of which it is a Constituent Entity, on or before the date specified in Article 5, if the following criteria are satisfied:

(i) the entity is resident for tax purposes in [Country]; and

(ii) one of the following conditions applies:

a) the Ultimate Parent Entity of the MNE Group is not obligated to file a Country-by-Country Report in its jurisdiction of tax residence; or,

b) the jurisdiction in which the Ultimate Parent Entity is resident for tax purposes has a current International Agreement to which [Country] is a party but does not have a Qualifying Competent Authority Agreement in effect to which [Country] is a party by the time specified in Article 5 for filing the Country-by-Country Report for the Reporting Fiscal Year; or,

c) there has been a Systemic Failure of the jurisdiction of tax residence of the Ultimate Parent Entity that has been notified by the [Country Tax Administration] to the Constituent Entity resident for tax purposes in [Country].

Where there are more than one Constituent Entities of the same MNE Group that are resident for tax purposes in [Country] and one or more of the conditions set out in subsection (ii) above apply, the MNE Group may designate one of such Constituent Entities to file the Country-by-Country Report conforming to the requirements of Article 4 with [Country Tax Administration] with respect to any Reporting Fiscal Year on or before the date specified in Article 5 and to notify the [Country Tax Administration] that the filing is intended to satisfy the filing requirement of all the Constituent Entities of such MNE Group that are resident for tax purposes in [Country].

3. Notwithstanding the provisions of paragraph 2 of this Article 2, when one or more of the conditions set out in subsection (ii) of paragraph 2 of Article 2 apply, an entity described in paragraph 2 of this Article 2 shall not be required to file a Country-by-Country Report with [Country Tax Administration] with respect to any Reporting Fiscal Year if the MNE Group of which it is a Constituent Entity has made available a Country-by-Country Report conforming to the requirements of Article 4 with respect to such Fiscal Year through a Surrogate Parent Entity that files that Country-by-Country Report with the tax authority of its jurisdiction of tax residence on or before the date specified in Article 5 and that satisfies the following conditions:

a) the jurisdiction of tax residence of the Surrogate Parent Entity requires filing of Country-by-Country Reports conforming to the requirements of Article 4;

b) the jurisdiction of tax residence of the Surrogate Parent Entity has a Qualifying Competent Authority Agreement in effect to which [Country] is a party by the time specified in Article 5 for filing the Country-by-Country Report for the Reporting Fiscal Year;

c) the jurisdiction of tax residence of the Surrogate Parent Entity has not notified the [Country Tax Administration] of a Systemic Failure;

d) the jurisdiction of tax residence of the Surrogate Parent Entity has been notified in accordance with paragraph 1 of Article 3 by the Constituent Entity resident for tax purposes in its jurisdiction that it is the Surrogate Parent Entity; and

e) a notification has been provided to [Country Tax Administration] in accordance with paragraph 2 of Article 3.

Article 3
Notification

1. Any Constituent Entity of an MNE Group that is resident for tax purposes in [Country] shall notify the [Country Tax Administration] whether it is the Ultimate Parent Entity or the Surrogate Parent Entity, no later than [the last day of the Reporting Fiscal Year of such MNE Group].

2. Where a Constituent Entity of an MNE Group that is resident for tax purposes in [Country] is not the Ultimate Parent Entity nor the Surrogate Parent Entity, it shall notify the [Country Tax Administration] of the identity and tax residence of the Reporting Entity, no later than [the last day of the Reporting Fiscal Year of such MNE Group].

Article 4
Country-by-Country Report

1. For purposes of this [title of the law], a Country-by-Country Report with respect to an MNE Group is a report containing:

(i) Aggregate information relating to the amount of revenue, profit (loss) before income tax, income tax paid, income tax accrued, stated capital, accumulated earnings, number of employees, and tangible assets other than cash or cash equivalents with regard to each jurisdiction in which the MNE Group operates;

(ii) An identification of each Constituent Entity of the MNE Group setting out the jurisdiction of tax residence of such Constituent Entity, and where different from such jurisdiction of tax residence, the jurisdiction under the laws of which such Constituent Entity is organised, and the nature of the main business activity or activities of such Constituent Entity.

2. The Country-by-Country Report shall be filed in a form identical to and applying the definitions and instructions contained in the standard template set out at [Annex III of Chapter V of the OECD Transfer Pricing Guidelines as the same may be modified from time to time] / [Annex III of the Report *Transfer Pricing Documentation and Country-by-Country Reporting* on Action 13 of the OECD/G20 *Action Plan on Base Erosion and Profit Shifting*] / [the Appendix to this law].

Article 5
Time for filing

The Country-by-Country Report required by this [title of the law] shall be filed no later than 12 months after the last day of the Reporting Fiscal Year of the MNE Group.

Article 6
Use and Confidentiality of Country-by-Country Report Information

1. The [Country Tax Administration] shall use the Country-by-Country Report for purposes of assessing high-level transfer pricing risks and other base erosion and profit shifting related risks in [Country], including assessing the risk of non-compliance by members of the MNE Group with applicable transfer pricing rules, and where appropriate for economic and statistical analysis. Transfer pricing adjustments by the [Country Tax Administration] will not be based on the CbC Report.

2. The [Country Tax Administration] shall preserve the confidentiality of the information contained in the Country-by-Country Report at least to the same extent that would apply if such information were provided to it under the provisions of the Multilateral Convention on Mutual Administrative Assistance in Tax Matters.

Article 7
Penalties

This model legislation does not include provisions regarding penalties to be imposed in the event a Reporting Entity fails to comply with the reporting requirements for the Country-by-Country Report. It is assumed that jurisdictions would wish to extend their existing transfer pricing documentation penalty regime to the requirements to file the Country-by-Country Report.

Article 8
Effective Date

This [title of the law] is effective for Reporting Fiscal Years of MNE Groups beginning on or after [1 January 2016].

Multilateral Competent Authority Agreement on the Exchange of Country-by-Country Reports

Whereas, the jurisdictions of the signatories to the Multilateral Competent Authority Agreement on the Exchange of Country-by-Country Reports (the "Agreement") are Parties of, or territories covered by, the Convention on Mutual Administrative Assistance in Tax Matters or the Convention on Mutual Administrative Assistance in Tax Matters as amended by the Protocol (the "Convention") or have signed or expressed their intention to sign the Convention and acknowledge that the Convention must be in force and in effect in relation to them before the automatic exchange of country-by-country (CbC) reports takes place;

Whereas, a country that has signed or expressed its intention to sign the Convention will only become a Jurisdiction as defined in Section 1 of this Agreement once it has become a Party to the Convention;

Whereas, the jurisdictions desire to increase international tax transparency and improve access of their respective tax authorities to information regarding the global allocation of the income, the taxes paid, and certain indicators of the location of economic activity among tax jurisdictions in which Multinational Enterprise (MNE) Groups operate through the automatic exchange of annual CbC Reports, with a view to assessing high-level transfer pricing risks and other base erosion and profit shifting related risks, as well as for economic and statistical analysis, where appropriate;

Whereas, the laws of the respective Jurisdictions require or are expected to require the Reporting Entity of an MNE Group to annually file a CbC Report;

Whereas, the CbC Report is intended to be part of a three-tiered structure, along with a global master file and a local file, which together represent a standardised approach to transfer pricing documentation which will provide tax administrations with relevant and reliable information to perform an efficient and robust transfer pricing risk assessment analysis;

Whereas, Chapter III of the Convention authorises the exchange of information for tax purposes, including the exchange of information on an automatic basis, and allows the competent authorities of the Jurisdictions to agree on the scope and modalities of such automatic exchanges;

Whereas, Article 6 of the Convention provides that two or more Parties can mutually agree to exchange information automatically, albeit that the actual exchange of the information will take place on a bilateral basis between the Competent Authorities;

Whereas, the Jurisdictions will have, or are expected to have, in place by the time the first exchange of CbC Reports takes place, (i) appropriate safeguards to ensure that the information received pursuant to this Agreement remains confidential and is used for the purposes of assessing high-level transfer pricing risks and other base erosion and profit shifting related risks, as well as for economic and statistical analysis, where appropriate, in accordance with Section 5 of this Agreement, (ii) the infrastructure for an effective exchange relationship (including established processes for ensuring timely, accurate, and confidential information exchanges, effective and reliable communications, and capabilities to promptly resolve questions and concerns about exchanges or requests for exchanges and to administer the provisions of Section 4 of this Agreement) and (iii) the necessary legislation to require Reporting Entities to file the CbC Report;

Whereas, the Jurisdictions are committed to discuss with the aim of resolving cases of undesirable economic outcomes, including for individual businesses, in accordance with paragraph 2 of Article 24 of the Convention, as well as paragraph 1 of Section 6 of this Agreement;

Whereas, mutual agreement procedures, for instance on the basis of a double tax convention concluded between the jurisdictions of the Competent Authorities, remain applicable in cases where the CbC Report has been exchanged on the basis of this Agreement;

Whereas, the Competent Authorities of the jurisdictions intend to conclude this Agreement, without prejudice to national legislative procedures (if any), and subject to the confidentiality and other protections provided for in the Convention, including the provisions limiting the use of the information exchanged thereunder;

Now, therefore, the Competent Authorities have agreed as follows:

SECTION 1
Definitions

1. For the purposes of this Agreement, the following terms have the following meanings:

a) the term **"Jurisdiction"** means a country or a territory in respect of which the Convention is in force and is in effect, either through ratification, acceptance or approval in accordance with Article 28, or through territorial extension in accordance with Article 29, and which is a signatory to this Agreement;

b) the term **"Competent Authority"** means, for each respective Jurisdiction, the persons and authorities listed in Annex B of the Convention;

c) The term **"Group"** means a collection of enterprises related through ownership or control such that it is either required to prepare consolidated financial statements for financial reporting purposes under applicable accounting principles or would be so required if equity interests in any of the enterprises were traded on a public securities exchange;

d) the term **"Multinational Enterprise (MNE) Group"** means any Group that (i) includes two or more enterprises the tax residence for which is in different jurisdictions, or includes an enterprise that is resident for tax purposes in one jurisdiction and is subject to tax with respect to the business carried out through a permanent establishment in another jurisdiction, and (ii) is not an Excluded MNE Group;

e) the term **"Excluded MNE Group"** means a Group that is not required to file a CbC Report on the basis that the annual consolidated group revenue of the Group during the fiscal year immediately preceding the reporting fiscal year, as reflected in its consolidated financial statements for such preceding fiscal year, is below the threshold defined in domestic law by the Jurisdiction and being consistent with the 2015 Report, as may be amended following the 2020 review contemplated therein;

f) the term **"Constituent Entity"** means (i) any separate business unit of an MNE Group that is included in the consolidated financial statements for financial reporting purposes, or would be so included if equity interests in such business unit of an MNE Group were traded on a public securities exchange, (ii) any separate business unit that is excluded from the MNE Group's consolidated financial statements solely on size or materiality grounds and (iii) any permanent establishment of any separate business unit of the MNE Group included in (i) or (ii) above provided the business unit prepares a separate financial statement for such permanent establishment for financial reporting, regulatory, tax reporting or internal management control purposes;

g) the term **"Reporting Entity"** means the Constituent Entity that, by virtue of domestic law in its jurisdiction of tax residence, files the CbC Report in its capacity to do so on behalf of the MNE Group;

h) the term **"CbC Report"** means the Country-by-Country Report to be filed annually by the Reporting Entity in accordance with the laws of its jurisdiction of tax residence and with the information required to be reported under such laws covering the items and reflecting the format set out in the 2015 Report, as may be amended following the 2020 review contemplated therein;

i) the term **"2015 Report"** means the consolidated report, entitled *Transfer Pricing Documentation and Country-by-Country Reporting*, on Action 13 of the OECD/G20 *Action Plan on Base Erosion and Profit Shifting*;

j) the term "**Co-ordinating Body**" means the co-ordinating body of the Convention that, pursuant to paragraph 3 of Article 24 of the Convention, is composed of representatives of the competent authorities of the Parties to the Convention;

k) the term **"Co-ordinating Body Secretariat"** means the OECD Secretariat that, pursuant to paragraph 3 of Article 24 of the Convention, provides support to the Co-ordinating Body;

l) the term **"Agreement in effect"** means, in respect of any two Competent Authorities, that both Competent Authorities have indicated their intention to automatically exchange information with each other and have satisfied the other conditions set out in paragraph 2 of Section 8. A list of Competent Authorities between which this Agreement is in effect is to be published on the OECD website.

2. As regards the application of this Agreement at any time by a Competent Authority of a Jurisdiction, any term not otherwise defined in this Agreement will, unless the context otherwise requires or the Competent Authorities agree to a common meaning (as permitted by domestic law), have the meaning that it has at that time under the law of the Jurisdiction applying this Agreement, any meaning under the applicable tax laws of that Jurisdiction prevailing over a meaning given to the term under other laws of that Jurisdiction.

SECTION 2

Exchange of Information with Respect to MNE Groups

1. Pursuant to the provisions of Articles 6, 21 and 22 of the Convention, each Competent Authority will annually exchange on an automatic basis the CbC Report received from each Reporting Entity that is resident for tax purposes in its jurisdiction with all such other Competent Authorities of Jurisdictions with respect to which it has this Agreement in effect, and in which, on the basis of the information in the CbC Report, one

or more Constituent Entities of the MNE Group of the Reporting Entity are either resident for tax purposes, or are subject to tax with respect to the business carried out through a permanent establishment.

2. Notwithstanding the previous paragraph, the Competent Authorities of the Jurisdictions that have indicated that they are to be listed as non-reciprocal jurisdictions on the basis of their notification pursuant to paragraph 1 b) of Section 8 will send CbC Reports pursuant to paragraph 1, but will not receive CbC Reports under this Agreement. Competent Authorities of Jurisdictions that are not listed as non-reciprocal Jurisdictions will both send and receive the information specified in paragraph 1. Competent Authorities will, however, not send such information to Competent Authorities of the Jurisdictions included in the aforementioned list of non-reciprocal Jurisdictions.

SECTION 3
Time and Manner of Exchange of Information

1. For the purposes of the exchange of information in Section 2, the currency of the amounts contained in the CbC Report will be specified.

2. With respect to paragraph 1 of Section 2, a CbC Report is first to be exchanged, with respect to the fiscal year of the MNE Group commencing on or after the date indicated by the Competent Authority in the notification pursuant to paragraph 1a) of Section 8, as soon as possible and no later than 18 months after the last day of that fiscal year. Notwithstanding the foregoing, a CbC Report is only required to be exchanged, if both Competent Authorities have this Agreement in effect and their respective Jurisdictions have in effect legislation that requires the filing of CbC Reports with respect to the fiscal year to which the CbC Report relates and that is consistent with the scope of exchange provided for in Section 2.

3. Subject to paragraph 2, the CbC Report is to be exchanged as soon as possible and no later than 15 months after the last day of the fiscal year of the MNE Group to which the CbC Report relates.

4. The Competent Authorities will automatically exchange the CbC Reports through a common schema in Extensible Markup Language.

5. The Competent Authorities will work towards and agree on one or more methods for electronic data transmission, including encryption standards, with a view to maximising standardisation and minimising complexities and costs and will notify the Co-ordinating Body Secretariat of such standardised transmission and encryption methods.

SECTION 4
Collaboration on Compliance and Enforcement

A Competent Authority will notify the other Competent Authority when the first-mentioned Competent Authority has reason to believe, with respect to a Reporting Entity that is resident for tax purposes in the jurisdiction of the other Competent Authority, that an error may have led to incorrect or incomplete information reporting or that there is non-compliance of a Reporting Entity with respect to its obligation to file a CbC Report. The notified Competent Authority will take appropriate measures available under its domestic law to address the errors or non-compliance described in the notice.

SECTION 5
Confidentiality, Data Safeguards and Appropriate Use

1. All information exchanged is subject to the confidentiality rules and other safeguards provided for in the Convention, including the provisions limiting the use of the information exchanged.

2. In addition to the restrictions in paragraph 1, the use of the information will be further limited to the permissible uses described in this paragraph. In particular, information received by means of the CbC Report will be used for assessing high-level transfer pricing, base erosion and profit shifting related risks, and, where appropriate, for economic and statistical analysis. The information will not be used as a substitute for a detailed transfer pricing analysis of individual transactions and prices based on a full functional analysis and a full comparability analysis. It is acknowledged that information in the CbC Report on its own does not constitute conclusive evidence that transfer prices are or are not appropriate and, consequently, transfer pricing adjustments will not be based on the CbC Report. Inappropriate adjustments in contravention of this paragraph made by local tax administrations will be conceded in any competent authority proceedings. Notwithstanding the above, there is no prohibition on using the CbC Report data as a basis for making further enquiries into the MNE Group's transfer pricing arrangements or into other tax matters in the course of a tax audit and, as a result, appropriate adjustments to the taxable income of a Constituent Entity may be made.

3. To the extent permitted under applicable law, a Competent Authority will notify the Co-ordinating Body Secretariat immediately of any cases of non-compliance with paragraphs 1 and 2 of this Section, including any remedial actions, as well as any measures taken in respect of non-compliance with the above-mentioned paragraphs. The Co-ordinating Body Secretariat will notify all Competent Authorities with respect to which this is an Agreement in effect with the first-mentioned Competent Authority.

SECTION 6
Consultations

1. In case an adjustment of the taxable income of a Constituent Entity, as a result of further enquiries based on the data in the CbC Report, leads to undesirable economic outcomes, including if such cases arise for a specific business, the Competent Authorities of the Jurisdictions in which the affected Constituent Entities are resident shall consult each other and discuss with the aim of resolving the case.

2. If any difficulties in the implementation or interpretation of this Agreement arise, a Competent Authority may request consultations with one or more of the Competent Authorities to develop appropriate measures to ensure that this Agreement is fulfilled. In particular, a Competent Authority shall consult with the other Competent Authority, before the first-mentioned Competent Authority determines that there is a systemic failure to exchange CbC Reports with the other Competent Authority. Where the first mentioned Competent Authority makes such a determination it shall notify the Co-ordinating Body Secretariat which, after having informed the other Competent Authority concerned, will notify all Competent Authorities. To the extent permitted by applicable law, either Competent Authority may, and if it so wishes through the Co-ordinating Body Secretariat, involve other Competent Authorities that have this Agreement in effect with a view to finding an acceptable resolution to the issue.

3. The Competent Authority that requested the consultations pursuant to paragraph 2 shall ensure, as appropriate, that the Co-ordinating Body Secretariat is notified of any conclusions that were reached and measures that were developed, including the absence of such conclusions or measures, and the Co-ordinating Body Secretariat will notify all Competent Authorities, even those that did not participate in the consultations, of any such conclusions or measures. Taxpayer-specific information, including information that would reveal the identity of the taxpayer involved, is not to be furnished.

SECTION 7
Amendments

This Agreement may be amended by consensus by written agreement of all of the Competent Authorities that have the Agreement in effect. Unless otherwise agreed upon, such an amendment is effective on the first day of the month following the expiration of a period of one month after the date of the last signature of such written agreement.

SECTION 8
Term of Agreement

1. A Competent Authority must provide, at the time of signature of this Agreement or as soon as possible thereafter, a notification to the Co-ordinating Body Secretariat:

a) that its Jurisdiction has the necessary laws in place to require Reporting Entities to file a CbC Report and that its Jurisdiction will require the filing of CbC Reports with respect to fiscal years of Reporting Entities commencing on or after the date set out in the notification;

b) specifying whether the Jurisdiction is to be included in the list of non-reciprocal Jurisdictions;

c) specifying one or more methods for electronic data transmission including encryption;

d) that it has in place the necessary legal framework and infrastructure to ensure the required confidentiality and data safeguards standards in accordance with Article 22 of the Convention and paragraph 1 and Section 5 of this Agreement, as well as the appropriate use of the information in the CbC Reports as described in paragraph 2 of Section 5 of this Agreement, and attaching the completed confidentiality and data safeguard questionnaire attached as Annex to this Agreement; and

e) that includes (i) a list of the Jurisdictions of the Competent Authorities with respect to which it intends to have this Agreement in effect, following national legislative procedures for entry into force (if any) or (ii) a declaration by the Competent Authority that it intends to have this Agreement in effect with all other Competent Authorities that provide a notification under paragraph 1e) of Section 8.

Competent Authorities must notify the Co-ordinating Body Secretariat, promptly, of any subsequent change to be made to any of the above-mentioned content of the notification.

2. This Agreement will come into effect between two Competent Authorities on the later of the following dates: (i) the date on which the second of the two Competent Authorities has provided notification to the Co-ordinating Body Secretariat under

paragraph 1 that includes the other Competent Authority's Jurisdiction pursuant to subparagraph 1e) and (ii) the date on which the Convention has entered into force and is in effect for both Jurisdictions.

3. The Co-ordinating Body Secretariat will maintain a list that will be published on the OECD website of the Competent Authorities that have signed the Agreement and between which Competent Authorities this is an Agreement in effect. In addition, the Co-ordinating Body Secretariat will publish the information provided by Competent Authorities pursuant to subparagraphs 1a) and b) on the OECD website.

4. The information provided pursuant to subparagraphs 1c) through e) will be made available to other signatories upon request in writing to the Co-ordinating Body Secretariat.

5. A Competent Authority may temporarily suspend the exchange of information under this Agreement by giving notice in writing to another Competent Authority that it has determined that there is or has been significant non-compliance by the second-mentioned Competent Authority with this Agreement. Before making such a determination, the first-mentioned Competent Authority shall consult with the other Competent Authority. For the purposes of this paragraph, significant non-compliance means non-compliance with paragraphs 1 and 2 of Section 5 and paragraph 1 of Section 6 of this Agreement and/ or the corresponding provisions of the Convention, as well as a failure by the Competent Authority to provide timely or adequate information as required under this Agreement. A suspension will have immediate effect and will last until the second-mentioned Competent Authority establishes in a manner acceptable to both Competent Authorities that there has been no significant non-compliance or that the second-mentioned Competent Authority has adopted relevant measures that address the significant non-compliance. To the extent permitted by applicable law, either Competent Authority may, and if it so wishes through the Co-ordinating Body Secretariat, involve other Competent Authorities that have this Agreement in effect with a view to finding an acceptable resolution to the issue.

6. A Competent Authority may terminate its participation in this Agreement, or with respect to a particular Competent Authority, by giving notice of termination in writing to the Co-ordinating Body Secretariat. Such termination will become effective on the first day of the month following the expiration of a period of 12 months after the date of the notice of termination. In the event of termination, all information previously received under this Agreement will remain confidential and subject to the terms of the Convention.

SECTION 9
Co-ordinating Body Secretariat

Unless otherwise provided for in the Agreement, the Co-ordinating Body Secretariat will notify all Competent Authorities of any notifications that it has received under this Agreement and will provide a notice to all signatories of the Agreement when a new Competent Authority signs the Agreement.

Done in English and French, both texts being equally authentic.

Annex to the Agreement – Confidentiality and Data Safeguards Questionnaire

1. Legal Framework

A legal framework must ensure the confidentiality of exchanged tax information and limit its use to appropriate purposes. The two basic components of such a framework are the terms of the applicable treaty, Tax Information Exchange Agreement (TIEA) or other bilateral agreement for the exchange of information, and a jurisdiction's domestic legislation.

1.1 Tax Conventions, TIEAs & Other Exchange Agreements	
Primary Check-list Areas	• Provisions in tax treaties, TIEAs and international agreements requiring confidentiality of exchanged information and restricting use to intended purposes
How do the exchange of information provisions in your Tax Conventions, TIEAs, or other exchange agreements ensure confidentiality and restrict the use of both outgoing information to other Contracting States and incoming information received in response to a request?	
1.2 Domestic Legislation	
Primary Check-list Areas	• Domestic law must apply safeguards to taxpayer information exchanged pursuant to a treaty, TIEA or other international agreement, and treat those information exchange agreements as binding, restrict data access and use and impose penalties for violations.
How do your domestic laws and regulations safeguard and restrict the use of information exchanged for tax purposes under Tax Conventions, TIEAs, or other exchange instruments? How does the tax administration prevent the misuse of confidential data and prohibit the transfer of tax information from the tax administrative body to non-tax government bodies?	

2. Information Security Management

The information security management systems used by each jurisdiction's tax administration must adhere to standards that ensure the protection of confidential taxpayer data. For example, there must be a screening process for employees handling the information, limits on who can access the information, and systems to detect and trace unauthorized disclosures. The internationally accepted standards for information security are known as the "ISO/IEC 27000-series". As described more fully below, a tax administration should be able to document that it is compliant with the ISO/IEC 27000-series standards or that it has an equivalent information security framework and that taxpayer information obtained under an exchange agreement is protected under that framework.

2.1.1 Background Checks and Contracts	
Primary Check-list Areas	• Screenings and background investigations for employees and contractors • Hiring process and contracts • Responsible Points of Contact
What procedures govern your tax administration's background investigations for employees and contractors who may have access to, use, or are responsible for protecting data received through exchange of information? Is this information publicly available? If so, please provide the reference. If not, please provide a summary of the procedures.	
2.1.2 Training and Awareness	
Primary Check-list Areas	• Initial training and periodic security awareness training based on roles, security risks, and applicable laws
What training does your tax administration provide to employees and contractors regarding confidential information including data received from partners through the Exchange of Information? Does your tax administration maintain a public version of the requirements? If so, please provide the reference. If not, please provide a summary of the requirement. [/End	
2.1.3 Departure Policies	
Primary Check-list Areas	• Departure policies to terminate access to confidential information
What procedures does your tax administration maintain for terminating access to confidential information for departing employees and consultants? Are the procedures publicly available? If so, please provide the reference. If not, please provide a summary of the procedures.	
2.2.1 Physical Security: Access to Premises	
Primary Check-list Areas	• Security measures to restrict entry to premises: security guards, policies, entry access procedures
What procedures does your tax administration maintain to grant employees, consultants, and visitors access to premises where confidential information, paper or electronic, is stored? Are the procedures publicly available? If so, please provide the reference. If not, please provide a summary of the procedures.	
2.2.2 Physical Security: Physical Document Storage	
Primary Check-list Areas	• Secure physical storage for confidential documents: policies and procedures
What procedures does your tax administration maintain for receiving, processing, archiving, retrieving and disposing of hard copies of confidential data received from taxpayers or exchange of information partners? Does your tax administration maintain procedures employees must follow when leaving their workspace at the end of the day? Are these procedures publicly available? If yes, please provide the reference. If not, please provide a summary. **Does your tax administration have a data classification policy? If so, please describe how your document storage procedures differ for data at all classification levels. Are these procedures publicly available? If yes, please provide the reference. If not, please provide a summary. [/End**	
2.3 Planning	
Primary Check-list Areas	• Planning documentation to develop, update, and implement security information systems
What procedures does your tax administration maintain to develop, document, update, and implement security for information systems used to receive, process, archive and retrieve confidential information? Are these procedures publicly available? If yes, please provide the reference. If not, please provide a summary. **What procedures does your tax administration maintain regarding periodic Information Security Plan updates to address changes to the information systems environment, and how are problems and risks identified during the implementation of Information Security Plans resolved? Are these procedures publicly available? If yes, please provide the reference. If not, please provide a summary.**	

2.4 Configuration Management	
Primary Check-list Areas	• Configuration management and security controls
What policies does your tax administration maintain to regulate system configuration and updates? Are the policies publicly available? If yes, please provide the reference. If not, please provide a summary. [/End question]	

2.5 Access Control	
Primary Check-list Areas	• Access Control Policies and procedures: authorized personnel and international exchange of information
What policies does your tax administration maintain to limit system access to authorized users and safeguard data during transmission when received and stored? Please describe how your tax administration's access authorization and data transmission policies extend to data received from an exchange of information partner under a treaty or TIEA or other exchange agreement. Are the policies publicly available? If yes, please provide the reference. If not, please provide a summary.	

2.6 Identification and Authentication	
Primary Check-list Areas	• Authenticating the identifying users and devices that require access to information systems
What policies and procedures does your tax administration maintain for each information system connected to confidential data? Are the policies and procedures publicly available? If so, please provide a reference. If not, please provide a summary. **What policies and procedures govern the authentication of authorized tax administration users by systems connected to confidential data? Are the policies and procedures publicly available? If so, please provide a reference. If not, please provide a summary.**	

2.7 Audit and Accountability	
Primary Check-list Areas	• Traceable electronic actions within systems • System audit procedures: monitoring, analyzing, investigating, and reporting of unlawful/ unauthorized use
What policies and procedures does your tax administration maintain to ensure system audits take place that will detect unauthorized access? Are the policies publicly available? If so, please provide a reference. If not, please provide a summary.	

2.8 Maintenance	
Primary Check-list Areas	• Periodic and timely maintenance of systems • Controls over: tools, procedures, and mechanisms for system maintenance and personnel use
What policies govern effective periodic system maintenance by your tax administration? Are these policies publicly available? If so, please provide a reference. If not, please provide a summary. **What procedures govern the resolution of system flaws identified by your tax administration? Are these procedures publicly available? If so, please provide a reference. If not, please provide a summary.**	

2.9 System and Communications Protection	
Primary Check-list Areas	• Procedures to monitor, control, and protect communications to and from information systems
What policies and procedures does your tax administration maintain for the electronic transmission and receipt of confidential data. Please describe the security and encryption requirements addressed in these policies. Are these policies publicly available? If so, please provide a reference. If not, please provide a summary.	

2.10 System and Information Integrity	
Primary Check-list Areas	• Procedures to identify, report, and correct information system flaws in a timely manner • Protection against malicious code and monitoring system security alerts
What procedures does your tax administration maintain to identify, report, and correct information system flaws in a timely manner? Please describe how these procedures provide for the protection of systems against malicious codes causing harm to data integrity. Are these procedures publicly available? If so, please provide a reference. If not, please provide a summary.	
2.11 Security Assessments	
Primary Check-list Areas	• Processes used to test, validate, and authorize the security controls for protecting data, correcting deficiencies, and reducing vulnerabilities
What policies does your tax administration maintain and regularly update for reviewing the processes used to test, validate, and authorize a security control plan? Is the policy publicly available? If so, please provide a reference. If not, please provide a summary.	
2.12 Contingency Planning	
Primary Check-list Areas	• Plans for emergency response, backup operations, and post-disaster recovery of information systems
What contingency plans and procedures does your tax administration maintain to reduce the impact of improper data disclosure or unrecoverable loss of data? Are the plans and procedures publicly available? If so, please provide a reference. If not, please provide a summary.	
2.13 Risk Assessment	
Primary Check-list Areas	• Potential risk of unauthorized access to taxpayer information • Risk and magnitude of harm from unauthorized use, disclosure, or disruption of the taxpayer information systems • Procedures to update risk assessment methodologies
Does your tax administration conduct risk assessments to identify risks and the potential impact of unauthorized access, use, and disclosure of information, or destruction of information systems? What procedures does your tax administration maintain to update risk assessment methodologies? Are these risk assessments and policies publicly available? If so, please provide a reference. If not, please provide a summary.	
2.14 Systems and Services Acquisition	
Primary Check-list Areas	• Methods and processes to ensure third-party providers of information systems process, store, and transmit confidential information in accordance with computer security requirements
What process does your tax administration maintain to ensure third-party providers are applying appropriate security controls that are consistent with computer security requirements for confidential information? Are the processes publicly available? If so, please provide a reference. If not, please provide a summary.	
2.15 Media Protection	
Primary Check-list Areas	• Processes to protect information in printed or digital form • Security measures used to limit media information access to authorized users only • Methods for sanitizing or destroying digital media prior to disposal or reuse
What processes does your tax administration maintain to securely store and limit access to confidential information in printed or digital form upon receipt from any source? How does your tax administration securely destroy confidential media information prior to its disposal? Are the processes available publicly? If so, please provide a reference. If not, please provide a summary.	

2.16 Protection of Treaty-Exchanged data (formerly Prevention of Data Commingling)	
Primary Check-list Areas	• Procedures to ensure treaty-exchanged files are safeguarded and clearly labeled • Classification methods of treaty-exchanged files
What policies and processes does your tax administration maintain to store confidential information and clearly label it as treaty-exchanged after receipt from foreign Competent Authorities? Are these policies and processes publicly available? If so, please provide a reference. If not, please provide a summary.	
2.17 Information Disposal Policies	
Primary Check-list Areas	• Procedures for properly disposing paper and electronic files
What procedures does your tax administration maintain for the disposal of confidential information? Do these procedures extend to exchanged information from foreign Competent Authorities? Are the procedures publicly available? If so, please provide a reference. If not, please provide a summary.	

3. Monitoring and Enforcement

In addition to keeping treaty-exchanged information confidential, tax administrations must be able to ensure that its use will be limited to the purposes defined by the applicable information exchange agreement. Thus, compliance with an acceptable information security framework alone is not sufficient to protect treaty-exchanged tax data. In addition, domestic law must impose penalties or sanctions for improper disclosure or use of taxpayer information. To ensure implementation, such laws must be reinforced by adequate administrative resources and procedures.

3.1 Penalties and Sanctions	
Primary Check-list Areas	• Penalties imposed for unauthorized disclosures • Risk mitigation practices
Does your tax administration have the ability to impose penalties for unauthorized disclosures of confidential information? Do the penalties extend to unauthorized disclosure of confidential information exchanged with a treaty or TIEA partner? Are the penalties publicly available? If so, please provide a reference. If not, please provide a summary.	
3.2.1 Policing Unauthorized Access and Disclosure	
Primary Check-list Areas	• Monitoring to detect breaches • Reporting of breaches
What procedures does your tax administration have to monitor confidentiality breaches? What policies and procedures does your tax administration have that require employees and contractors to report actual or potential breaches of confidentiality? What reports does your tax administration prepare when a breach of confidentiality occurs? Are these policies and procedures publicly available? If so, please provide a reference. If not, please provide a summary.	
3.2.2 Sanctions and Prior Experience	
Primary Check-list Areas	• Prior unauthorized disclosures • Policy/process modifications to prevent future breaches
Have there been any cases in your jurisdiction where confidential information has been improperly disclosed? Have there been any cases in your jurisdiction where confidential information received by the Competent Authority from an exchange of information partner has been disclosed other than in accordance with the terms of the instrument under which it was provided? Does your tax administration or Inspector General make available to the public descriptions of any breaches, any penalties/sanctions imposed, and changes put in place to mitigate risk and prevent future breaches? If so, please provide a reference. If not, please provide a summary.	

Competent Authority Agreement on the Exchange of Country-by-Country Reports on the basis of a Double Tax Convention ("DTC CAA")

Whereas, the Government of [Jurisdiction A] and the Government of [Jurisdiction B] desire to increase international tax transparency and improve access of their respective tax authorities to information regarding the global allocation of the income, the taxes paid, and certain indicators of the location of economic activity among tax jurisdictions in which Multinational Enterprise (MNE) Groups operate through the automatic exchange of annual CbC Reports, with a view to assessing high-level transfer pricing risks and other base erosion and profit shifting related risks, as well as for economic and statistical analysis, where appropriate;

Whereas, the laws of their respective Jurisdictions require or are expected to require the Reporting Entity of an MNE Group to annually file a CbC Report;

Whereas, the CbC Report is intended to be part of a three-tiered structure, along with a global master file and a local file, which together represent a standardised approach to transfer pricing documentation which will provide tax administrations with relevant and reliable information to perform an efficient and robust transfer pricing risk assessment analysis;

Whereas, Article [...] of the Income Tax Convention between [Jurisdiction A] and [Jurisdiction B] (the "Convention"), authorises the exchange of information for tax purposes, including the automatic exchange of information, and allows the competent authorities of [Jurisdiction A] and [Jurisdiction B] (the "Competent Authorities") to agree the scope and modalities of such automatic exchanges;

Whereas, [Jurisdiction A] and [Jurisdiction B] [have/are expected to have/have, or are expected to have,] in place by the time the first exchange of CbC Reports takes place (i) appropriate safeguards to ensure that the information received pursuant to this Agreement remains confidential and is used for the purposes of assessing high-level transfer pricing risks and other base erosion and profit shifting related risks, as well as for economic and statistical analysis, where appropriate, in accordance with Section 5 of this Agreement, (ii) the infrastructure for an effective exchange relationship (including established processes for ensuring timely, accurate, and confidential information exchanges, effective and reliable communications, and capabilities to promptly resolve questions and concerns about exchanges or requests for exchanges and to administer the provisions of Section 4 of this Agreement), and (iii) the necessary legislation to require Reporting Entities to file the CbC Report;

Whereas, [Jurisdiction A] and [Jurisdiction B] are committed to endeavour to mutually agree on resolving cases of double taxation in accordance with Article [25] of the Convention, as well as paragraph 1 of Section 6 of this Agreement;

Whereas, the Competent Authorities intend to conclude this Agreement on reciprocal automatic exchange pursuant to the Convention and subject to the confidentiality and other protections provided for in the Convention, including the provisions limiting the use of the information exchanged thereunder;

Now, therefore, the Competent Authorities have agreed as follows:

SECTION 1
Definitions

1. For the purposes of this Agreement, the following terms have the following meanings:

a) the term **"[Jurisdiction A]"** means [...];

b) the term **"[Jurisdiction B]"** means [...];

c) the term **"Competent Authority"** means in case of [Jurisdiction A], [...] and in case of [Jurisdiction B], [...];

d) The term "**Group**" means a collection of enterprises related through ownership or control such that it is either required to prepare consolidated financial statements for financial reporting purposes under applicable accounting principles or would be so required if equity interests in any of the enterprises were traded on a public securities exchange;

e) the term **"Multinational Enterprise (MNE) Group"** means any Group that (i) includes two or more enterprises the tax residence for which is in different jurisdictions, or includes an enterprise that is resident for tax purposes in one jurisdiction and is subject to tax with respect to the business carried out through a permanent establishment in another jurisdiction, and (ii) is not an Excluded MNE Group;

f) the term **"Excluded MNE Group"** means a Group that is not required to file a CbC Report on the basis that the consolidated group revenue of the Group during the fiscal year immediately preceding the reporting fiscal year, as reflected in its consolidated financial statements for such preceding fiscal year, is below the threshold defined in domestic law by the Jurisdiction and being consistent with the 2015 Report, as may be amended following the 2020 review contemplated therein;

g) the term **"Constituent Entity"** means (i) any separate business unit of an MNE Group that is included in the consolidated financial statements for financial reporting purposes, or would be so included if equity interests in such business unit of an MNE Group were traded on a public securities exchange (ii) any separate business unit that is excluded from the MNE Group's consolidated financial statements solely on size or materiality grounds and (iii) any permanent establishment of any separate business unit of the MNE Group included in (i) or (ii) above provided the business unit prepares a separate financial statement for such permanent establishment for financial reporting, regulatory, tax reporting or internal management control purposes;

h) the term **"Reporting Entity"** means the Constituent Entity that, by virtue of domestic law in its jurisdiction of tax residence, files the CbC Report in its capacity to do so on behalf of the MNE Group;

i) the term **"CbC Report"** means the Country-by-Country Report to be filed annually by the Reporting Entity in accordance with the laws of its jurisdiction of tax residence and with the information required to be reported under such laws covering the items and reflecting the format set out in the 2015 Report, as may be amended following the 2020 review contemplated therein; and

j) the term **"2015 Report"** means the consolidated report, entitled *Transfer Pricing Documentation and Country-by-Country Reporting*, on Action 13 of the OECD/ G20 *Action Plan on Base Erosion and Profit Shifting.*

2. As regards to the application of this Agreement at any time by a Competent Authority of a Jurisdiction, any term not otherwise defined in this Agreement will, unless the context otherwise requires or the Competent Authorities agree to a common meaning (as permitted by domestic law), have the meaning that it has at that time under the law of the Jurisdiction applying this Agreement, any meaning under the applicable tax laws of that Jurisdiction prevailing over a meaning given to the term under other laws of that Jurisdiction.

SECTION 2
Exchange of Information with Respect to MNE Groups

Pursuant to the provisions of Article [...] of the Convention, each Competent Authority will annually exchange on an automatic basis the CbC Report received from each Reporting Entity that is resident for tax purposes in its Jurisdiction with the other Competent Authority, provided that, on the basis of the information provided in the CbC Report, one or more Constituent Entities of the MNE Group of the Reporting Entity are resident for tax purposes in the Jurisdiction of the other Competent Authority or, are subject to tax with respect to the business carried out through a permanent establishment situated in the Jurisdiction of the other Competent Authority.

SECTION 3
Time and Manner of Exchange of Information

1. For the purposes of the exchange of information in Section 2, the currency of the amounts contained in the CbC Report will be specified.

2. With respect to Section 2, a CbC Report is first to be exchanged with respect to fiscal years of MNE Groups commencing on or after [...]. Such CbC Report is to be exchanged as soon as possible and no later than 18 months after the last day of the fiscal year of the MNE Group to which the CbC Report relates. CbC Reports with respect to subsequent fiscal years are to be exchanged as soon as possible and no later than 15 months after the last day of the fiscal year of the MNE Group to which the CbC Report relates.

3. The Competent Authorities will automatically exchange the CbC Reports through a common schema in Extensible Markup Language.

4. The Competent Authorities will work towards and agree on one or more methods for electronic data transmission including encryption standards.

SECTION 4
Collaboration on Compliance and Enforcement

A Competent Authority will notify the other Competent Authority when the first-mentioned Competent Authority has reason to believe, with respect to a Reporting Entity that is resident for tax purposes in the Jurisdiction of the other Competent Authority, that an error may have led to incorrect or incomplete information reporting or that there is non-compliance of a Reporting Entity with the respect to its obligation to file a CbC Report.

The notified Competent Authority will take all appropriate measures available under its domestic law to address the errors or non-compliance described in the notice.

SECTION 5
Confidentiality, Data Safeguards and Appropriate Use

1. All information exchanged is subject to the confidentiality rules and other safeguards provided for in the Convention, including the provisions limiting the use of the information exchanged.

2. In addition to the restrictions in paragraph 1, the use of the information will be further limited to the permissible uses described in this paragraph. In particular, information received by means of the CbC Report will be used for assessing high-level transfer pricing, base erosion and profit shifting related risks, and, where appropriate, for economic and statistical analysis. The information will not be used as a substitute for a detailed transfer pricing analysis of individual transactions and prices based on a full functional analysis and a full comparability analysis. It is acknowledged that information in the CbC Report on its own does not constitute conclusive evidence that transfer prices are or are not appropriate and, consequently, transfer pricing adjustments will not be based on the CbC Report. Inappropriate adjustments in contravention of this paragraph made by local tax administrations will be conceded in any competent authority proceedings. Notwithstanding the above, there is no prohibition on using the CbC Report data as a basis for making further enquiries into the MNE Group's transfer pricing arrangements or into other tax matters in the course of a tax audit and, as a result, appropriate adjustments to the taxable income of a Constituent Entity may be made.

3. To the extent permitted under applicable law, each Competent Authority will notify the other Competent Authority immediately regarding of any cases of non-compliance with the rules set out in paragraphs 1 and 2 of this Section, including any remedial actions, as well as any measures taken in respect of non-compliance with the above-mentioned paragraphs.

SECTION 6
Consultations

1. In cases foreseen by Article [25] of the Convention, the Competent Authorities of both Jurisdictions shall consult each other and endeavour to resolve the situation by mutual agreement.

2. If any difficulties in the implementation or interpretation of this Agreement arise, either Competent Authority may request consultations with the other Competent Authority to develop appropriate measures to ensure that this Agreement is fulfilled. In particular, a Competent Authority shall consult with the other Competent Authority before the first-mentioned Competent Authority determines that there is a systemic failure to exchange CbC Reports with the other Competent Authority.

SECTION 7
Amendments

This Agreement may be amended by consensus by written agreement of the Competent Authorities. Unless otherwise agreed upon, such an amendment is effective on the first day of the month following the expiration of a period of one month after the date of the last signature of such written agreement.

SECTION 8
Term of Agreement

1. This Agreement will come into effect on [.../the date of the later of the notifications provided by each Competent Authority that its Jurisdiction either has the necessary laws in place to require Reporting Entities to file a CbC Report].

2. A Competent Authority may temporarily suspend the exchange of information under this Agreement by giving notice in writing to the other Competent Authority that it has determined that there is or has been significant non-compliance by the other Competent Authority with this Agreement. Before making such a determination, the first-mentioned Competent Authority shall consult with the other Competent Authority. For the purposes of this paragraph, significant non-compliance means non-compliance with paragraphs 1 and 2 of Section 5 and paragraph 1 of Section 6 of this Agreement, including the provisions of the Convention referred to therein, as well as a failure by the Competent Authority to provide timely or adequate information as required under this Agreement. A suspension will have immediate effect and will last until the second-mentioned Competent Authority establishes in a manner acceptable to both Competent Authorities that there has been no significant non-compliance or that the second-mentioned Competent Authority has adopted relevant measures that address the significant non-compliance.

3. Either Competent Authority may terminate this Agreement by giving notice of termination in writing to the other Competent Authority. Such termination will become effective on the first day of the month following the expiration of a period of 12 months after the date of the notice of termination. In the event of termination, all information previously received under this Agreement will remain confidential and subject to the terms of the Convention.

Signed in duplicate in [...] on [...].

Competent Authority for [Jurisdiction A]	Competent Authority for [Jurisdiction B]

Competent Authority Agreement on the Exchange of Country-by-Country Reports on the basis of a Tax Information Exchange Agreement ("TIEA CAA")

Whereas, the Government of [Jurisdiction A] and the Government of [Jurisdiction B] intend to increase international tax transparency and improve access of their respective tax authorities to information regarding the global allocation of the income, the taxes paid, and certain indicators of the location of economic activity among tax jurisdictions in which Multinational Enterprise (MNE) Groups operate through the automatic exchange of annual CbC Reports, with a view to assessing high-level transfer pricing risks and other base erosion and profit shifting related risks, as well as for economic and statistical analysis, where appropriate;

Whereas, the laws of their respective Jurisdictions require or are expected to require the Reporting Entity of an MNE Group to annually file a CbC Report;

Whereas, the CbC Report is intended to be part of a three-tiered structure, along with a global master file and a local file, which together represent a standardised approach to transfer pricing documentation which will provide tax administrations with relevant and reliable information to perform an efficient and robust transfer pricing risk assessment analysis;

Whereas, Article [5A] of the Tax Information Exchange Agreement between [Jurisdiction A] and [Jurisdiction B] (the "TIEA"), authorises the exchange of information for tax purposes, including the automatic exchange of information, and allows the competent authorities of [Jurisdiction A] and [Jurisdiction B] (the "Competent Authorities") to agree the scope and modalities of such automatic exchanges;

Whereas, [Jurisdiction A] and [Jurisdiction B] [have/are expected to have/have, or are expected to have,] in place by the time the first exchange of CbC Reports takes place (i) appropriate safeguards to ensure that the information received pursuant to this Agreement remains confidential and is used for the purposes of assessing high-level transfer pricing risks and other base erosion and profit shifting related risks, as well as for economic and statistical analysis, where appropriate, in accordance with Section 5 of this Agreement, (ii) the infrastructure for an effective exchange relationship (including established processes for ensuring timely, accurate, and confidential information exchanges, effective and reliable communications, and capabilities to promptly resolve questions and concerns about exchanges or requests for exchanges and to administer the provisions of Section 4 of this Agreement) and (iii) the necessary legislation to require Reporting MNEs to file the CbC Report;

Whereas, the Competent Authorities intend to conclude this Agreement on reciprocal automatic exchange pursuant to the TIEA and subject to the confidentiality and other protections provided for in the TIEA, including the provisions limiting the use of the information exchanged thereunder;

Now, therefore, the Competent Authorities have agreed as follows:

SECTION 1
Definitions

1. For the purposes of this Agreement, the following terms have the following meanings:

a) the term **"[Jurisdiction A]"** means [...];

b) the term **"[Jurisdiction B]"** means [...];

c) the term **"Competent Authority"** means in case of [Jurisdiction A], [...] and in case of [Jurisdiction B], [...];

d) The term **"Group"** means a collection of enterprises related through ownership or control such that it is either required to prepare consolidated financial statements for financial reporting purposes under applicable accounting principles or would be so required if equity interests in any of the enterprises were traded on a public securities exchange;

e) the term **"Multinational Enterprise (MNE) Group"** means any Group that (i) includes two or more enterprises the tax residence for which is in different jurisdictions, or includes an enterprise that is resident for tax purposes in one jurisdiction and is subject to tax with respect to the business carried out through a permanent establishment in another jurisdiction, and (ii) is not an Excluded MNE Group;

f) the term **"Excluded MNE Group"** means a Group that is not required to file a CbC Report on the basis that the consolidated group revenue of the Group during the fiscal year immediately preceding the reporting fiscal year, as reflected in its consolidated financial statements for such preceding fiscal year, is below the threshold defined in domestic law by the Jurisdiction and being consistent with the 2015 Report, as may be amended following the 2020 review contemplated therein;

g) the term **"Constituent Entity"** means (i) any separate business unit of an MNE Group that is included in the consolidated financial statements for financial reporting purposes, or would be so included if equity interests in such business unit of an MNE Group were traded on a public securities exchange (ii) any separate business unit that is excluded from the MNE Group's consolidated financial statements solely on size or materiality grounds and (iii) any permanent establishments of any separate business unit of the MNE Group included in (i) or (ii) above provided such business unit prepares a separate financial statement for such permanent establishment for financial reporting, regulatory, tax reporting or internal management control purposes;

h) the term **"Reporting Entity"** means the Constituent Entity that, by virtue of domestic law in its jurisdiction of tax residence, files the CbC Report in its capacity to do so on behalf of the MNE Group;

i) the term **"CbC Report"** means the Country-by-Country Report to be filed annually by the Reporting Entity in accordance with the laws of its jurisdiction of tax residence and with the information required to be reported under such laws covering the items and reflecting the format set out in the 2015 Report, as may be amended following the 2020 review contemplated therein; and

j) the term **"2015 Report"** means the consolidated report, entitled *Transfer Pricing Documentation and Country-by-Country Reporting*, on Action 13 of the OECD/G20 *Action Plan on Base Erosion and Profit Shifting.*

2. As regards to the application of this Agreement at any time by a Competent Authority of a Jurisdiction, any term not otherwise defined in this Agreement will, unless the context otherwise requires or the Competent Authorities agree to a common meaning (as permitted by domestic law), have the meaning that it has at that time under the law of the Jurisdiction applying this Agreement, any meaning under the applicable tax laws of that Jurisdiction prevailing over a meaning given to the term under other laws of that Jurisdiction.

SECTION 2
Exchange of Information with Respect to MNE Groups

Pursuant to the provisions of Article [5A] of the TIEA, each Competent Authority will annually exchange on an automatic basis the CbC Report received from each Reporting Entity that is resident for tax purposes in its Jurisdiction with the other Competent Authority, provided that, on the basis of the information provided in the CbC Report, one or more Constituent Entities of the MNE Group of the Reporting Entity are resident for tax purposes in the Jurisdiction of the other Competent Authority or, are subject to tax with respect to the business carried out through a permanent establishment situated in the Jurisdiction of the other Competent Authority.

SECTION 3
Time and Manner of Exchange of Information

1. For the purposes of the exchange of information in Section 2, the currency of the amounts contained in the CbC Report will be specified.

2. With respect to Section 2, a CbC Report is first to be exchanged with respect to fiscal years of MNE Groups commencing on or after [...]. Such CbC Report is to be exchanged as soon as possible and no later than 18 months after the last day of the fiscal year of the Reporting Entity of the MNE Group to which the CbC Report relates. CbC Reports with respect to subsequent fiscal years are to be exchanged as soon as possible and no later than 15 months after the last day of the fiscal year of the MNE Group to which the CbC Report relates.

3. The Competent Authorities will automatically exchange the CbC Reports through a common schema in Extensible Markup Language.

4. The Competent Authorities will work towards and agree on one or more methods for electronic data transmission including encryption standards.

SECTION 4
Collaboration on Compliance and Enforcement

A Competent Authority will notify the other Competent Authority when the first-mentioned Competent Authority has reason to believe, with respect to a Reporting Entity that is resident for tax purposes in the Jurisdiction of the other Competent Authority, that an error may have led to incorrect or incomplete information reporting or that there is non-compliance of a Reporting Entity with the respect to its obligation to file a CbC Report.

The notified Competent Authority will take all appropriate measures available under its domestic law to address the errors or non-compliance described in the notice.

SECTION 5
Confidentiality, Data Safeguards and Appropriate Use

1. All information exchanged is subject to the confidentiality rules and other safeguards provided for in the TIEA, including the provisions limiting the use of the information exchanged.

2. In addition to the restrictions in paragraph 1, the use of the information will be further limited to the permissible uses described in this paragraph. In particular, information received by means of the CbC Report will be used for assessing high-level transfer pricing, base erosion and profit shifting related risks, and, where appropriate, for economic and statistical analysis. The information will not be used as a substitute for a detailed transfer pricing analysis of individual transactions and prices based on a full functional analysis and a full comparability analysis. It is acknowledged that information in the CbC Report on its own does not constitute conclusive evidence that transfer prices are or are not appropriate and, consequently, transfer pricing adjustments will not be based on the CbC Report. Inappropriate adjustments in contravention of this paragraph made by local tax administrations will be conceded in any competent authority proceedings. Notwithstanding the above, there is no prohibition on using the CbC Report data as a basis for making further enquiries into the MNE's transfer pricing arrangements or into other tax matters in the course of a tax audit and, as a result, appropriate adjustments to the taxable income of a Constituent Entity may be made.

3. To the extent permitted under applicable law, each Competent Authority will notify the other Competent Authority immediately regarding of any cases of non-compliance with the paragraphs 1 and 2 of this Section, including any remedial actions, as well as any measures taken in respect of non-compliance with the above-mentioned paragraphs.

SECTION 6
Consultations

1. In case an adjustment of the taxable income of a Constituent Entity, as a result of further enquiries based on the data in the CbC Report, leads to undesirable economic outcomes, including if such cases arise for a specific business, both Competent Authorities shall consult each other and discuss with the aim of resolving the case.

2. If any difficulties in the implementation or interpretation of this Agreement arise, either Competent Authority may request consultations with of the other Competent Authority to develop appropriate measures to ensure that this Agreement is fulfilled. In particular, a Competent Authority shall consult with the other Competent Authority before the first-mentioned Competent Authority determines that there is a systemic failure to exchange CbC Reports with the other Competent Authority.

SECTION 7
Amendments

This Agreement may be amended by consensus by written agreement of the Competent Authorities. Unless otherwise agreed upon, such an amendment is effective on the first day of the month following the expiration of a period of one month after the date of the last signature of such written agreement.

SECTION 8
Term of Agreement

1. This Agreement will come into effect on [.../the date of the later of the notifications provided by each Competent Authority that its Jurisdiction either has the necessary laws in place to require Reporting Entities to file a CbC Report].

2. A Competent Authority may temporarily suspend the exchange of information under this Agreement by giving notice in writing to the other Competent Authority that it has determined that there is or has been significant non-compliance by the other Competent Authority with this Agreement. Before making such a determination, the first-mentioned Competent Authority shall consult with the other Competent Authority. For the purposes of this paragraph, significant non-compliance means non-compliance with paragraphs 1 and 2 of Section 5 and paragraph 1 of Section 6 of this Agreement and the provisions of the TIEA referred to therein, as well as a failure by the Competent Authority to provide timely or adequate information as required under this Agreement. A suspension will have immediate effect and will last until the second-mentioned Competent Authority establishes in a manner acceptable to both Competent Authorities that there has been no significant non-compliance or that the second-mentioned Competent Authority has adopted relevant measures that address the significant non-compliance.

3. Either Competent Authority may terminate this Agreement by giving notice of termination in writing to the other Competent Authority. Such termination will become effective on the first day of the month following the expiration of a period of 12 months after the date of the notice of termination. In the event of termination, all information previously received under this Agreement will remain confidential and subject to the terms of the TIEA.

Signed in duplicate in [...] on [...].

Competent Authority for [Jurisdiction A]	Competent Authority for [Jurisdiction B]

Bibliography

OECD (2014), *Standard for Automatic Exchange of Financial Account Information in Tax Matters*, OECD Publishing, Paris, http://dx.doi.org/10.1787/9789264216525-en.

OECD (2013), *Action Plan on Base Erosion and Profit Shifting*, OECD Publishing, Paris, http://dx.doi.org/10.1787/9789264202719-en.

OECD (2012), *Keeping it Safe: The OECD Guide on the protection of confidentiality of information exchanged for tax purposes,* OECD Publishing, Paris, www.oecd.org/ctp/exchange-of-tax-information/keeping-it-safe-report.pdf.

OECD (2010), *OECD Transfer Pricing Guidelines for Multinational Enterprises and Tax Administrations 2010,* OECD Publishing, Paris, http://dx.doi.org/10.1787/tpg-2010-en.

ORGANISATION FOR ECONOMIC CO-OPERATION AND DEVELOPMENT

The OECD is a unique forum where governments work together to address the economic, social and environmental challenges of globalisation. The OECD is also at the forefront of efforts to understand and to help governments respond to new developments and concerns, such as corporate governance, the information economy and the challenges of an ageing population. The Organisation provides a setting where governments can compare policy experiences, seek answers to common problems, identify good practice and work to co-ordinate domestic and international policies.

The OECD member countries are: Australia, Austria, Belgium, Canada, Chile, the Czech Republic, Denmark, Estonia, Finland, France, Germany, Greece, Hungary, Iceland, Ireland, Israel, Italy, Japan, Korea, Luxembourg, Mexico, the Netherlands, New Zealand, Norway, Poland, Portugal, the Slovak Republic, Slovenia, Spain, Sweden, Switzerland, Turkey, the United Kingdom and the United States. The European Union takes part in the work of the OECD.

OECD Publishing disseminates widely the results of the Organisation's statistics gathering and research on economic, social and environmental issues, as well as the conventions, guidelines and standards agreed by its members.

OECD PUBLISHING, 2, rue André-Pascal, 75775 PARIS CEDEX 16
(23 2015 38 1 P) ISBN 978-92-64-24146-6 – 2015-07

www.ingramcontent.com/pod-product-compliance
Lightning Source LLC
LaVergne TN
LVHW081422110826
845149LV00010B/1833

9789264241466